To Mary—

In celibration of harmony
and balance.

Many blessings.

Carol Hyker

Wind and Water

Your Personal Feng Shui Journey

Carole J. Hyder

Hyder Enterprises

Minneapolis, Minnesota

Carole
Hyder

吾道不孤

青出於藍

一九九八年端午碌青持

無量咒以為

女弟風水宏著暨讀者闔府長幼

新福納財增慧袪病延壽保年安

佛門密宗黑教第三期院禪

林雲

時寫德國

慕尼黑

On the path of conveying the Tao, I am no longer solitude.
The color of indigo originates from the color blue.

Calligraphy by Professor Thomas Lin Yun

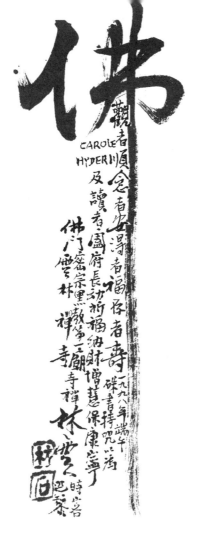

Buddha

Calligraphy by Professor Thomas Lin Yun

First printing.

Hyder Enterprises, 901 W. Minnehaha Parkway, Minneapolis MN 55419, 612-823-5093, hyder@goldengate.net

Book design by Dorie McClelland, Spring Type & Design

Photo credits:
Page 256: Warwick Greene
Back cover: Jason J. Jorgensen

Publisher's Cataloging-in-Publication
(Provided by Quality Books, Inc.)

Hyder, Carole J.
    Wind and water : your personal feng shui journey / Carole J. Hyder — 1st ed.
    p. cm.
    ISBN 0-9664434-0-3

    1. Feng-shui   I. Title.

    BF1779.F4H93 1998   133.3'337
                                QBI98-656

Dedication

To Master Thomas Lin Yun,
my teacher,
and
to all those who went before him,
with humble gratitude
from my heart

With regard to Feng Shui, the science of placement, the knowledge I have acquired is limited and the contribution I have made minimal. In retrospect, I have come to realize that a long time has elapsed between the period when I started at the age of sixteen or seventeen up to the present age of sixty-seven. During this period of time, I began by learning with gratitude from two well-respected masters, Cheng Kui-Ying in Roho province and Hui Chie-Fu in Shangtong province. Through practical application and empirical research, I am finally lecturing and teaching classes in Europe, America, Asia, Australia and other countries. This path has been over fifty years.

A Chinese proverb goes "teaching is learning." In my fifty years of learning, lecturing and teaching, I indeed have gained more profound knowledge from my students, disciples, audience, other gurus, specialists and scholars.

I, therefore, incorporate the essence of traditional Feng Shui of various schools, the Fourth Stage of Black Sect Tantric Buddhism and the complicated cultures of India, Tibet and mainland China. By integrating modern scientific knowledge, psychology, physiology, urban planning, etc., as well as some spiritual knowledge, I have initiated and established Feng Shui of Black Sect Tantric Buddhism.

This pioneering and unique school has given inspiration to the four valuable books written by Sarah Rossbach, who has followed my teaching and promoted and enunciated my theory for over twenty years. It has then been further spread by intelligent, loving and well-cultivated disciples such as Katherine Metz. The result is that not only are there many people in America and Europe showing great interest in the teachings of the school, but also many people providing classes, writing articles and publishing books. They have achieved success in various degrees, making more and greater contributions to society and humanity.

Among the works of special expertise, all with highest value in their own right, is added this most recent and most outstanding book enunciating the essence of Feng Shui entitled *Wind and Water: Your Personal Feng Shui Journey* by Carole J. Hyder.

In this book, the author begins by guiding us on how to use the book. We are guided from understanding the concept of Feng Shui, including the definition of the eight trigrams (the bagua) and visualization power, to analyzing the essential points of Feng Shui. Finally, the author discusses and analyzes the various practical ways to implement the precious and honorable Feng Shui knowledge into our daily working and living environments.

This book is full of unique points. It clearly informs and explains to its readers the principles of Feng Shui from the Black Sect Tantric Buddhism perspective, which originates from the Chinese tradition, but not limited to the traditional viewpoint. This school is based on modern science as well as my fifty years of practical Feng Shui experience.

The author's writing technique, editing of the contents and the order are very special and unconventional. Even readers who have never studied Feng Shui before will find it easy to grasp and to understand, and thus will be eager to try it. Readers who have studied Feng Shui will acquire new understanding by inducing and deducing from a different angle. By reviewing this book, everyone who reads it can attain a new way of evaluating life in the context of Feng Shui.

Lin Yun
May 1998

Translators: Allan Lin, Julia Hsu

Contents

Acknowledgements

The school of Feng Shui that I have studied and practiced since 1992 is Black Sect Tantric Buddhist Feng Shui. I am a disciple and student of Master Thomas Lin Yun, the man who is responsible for this form of Feng Shui. Professor Lin is a Buddhist teacher who lives in Berkeley, California, and teaches from the Yun Lin Temple. He has beautifully blended the traditional art of placement with the modern Western world without sacrificing any of the integrity of the ancient school. His evolutionary work with Feng Shui has made the concept adaptable into our homes and into our hearts. Professor Lin has enabled Feng Shui to become "user friendly" to a culture which, until a few years ago, had never heard the term. From his profound insights and those of Katherine Metz, a senior student of Professor Lin's for many years, I am where I am today.

My gratitude also goes to Barbara Bobrowitz, my business partner in Balanced Environment.™ We have traveled the Feng Shui path together since 1992, speaking from our hearts about Feng Shui to anyone who would ask.

I wasn't sure I had the makings of a book until my dear friend Vara Kamin read the beginning pages and declared it "real." Thanks to my readers Patti Baldwin, Barbara Gutkin, Carol Cannon, and Janet Sawyer. A special thanks to Judy Cigan Hall for her in-depth editing, comments, and cheerleading. And thank you to Robert and Diane Brown who "saw" the book before I did with their astrological eyes and, despite us being total strangers, reassured my hesitation around starting this endeavor.

To my sweet and constant feline companion, Muffin, whose wisdom and compassion inspired me many days when I didn't feel like writing. I'm sorry she didn't live to see the finished product.

Words cannot express enough gratitude to my designer, Dorie McClelland. A steady and persistent beacon, she kept me on track. Her cover design, her editing, her insights, and her organization enabled *Wind and Water: Your Personal Feng Shui Journey* to happen in a painless and exhilarating fashion. She brought the integrity and gentleness to this book for which I was searching. I extend heartfelt blessings and continued success to all of her endeavors.

Finally, to my husband, Tom, who not only read several versions of the manuscript with a loving and critical eye, but also allowed it to flow over into our lives. I'm grateful for his patience and his unwavering support to me around this project. He never once doubted my capabilities, and he mirrored that message to me more times than he'll ever realize. May Feng Shui continue to permeate our life together.

How to use this book

Just as Feng Shui can be accessed in a person's life on many levels of understanding and involvement, so too this book acquired the same structure. It can be read on a daily basis, one page or thought per day. At the end of the journey, you will have experienced Feng Shui as a day-by-day process that continues and begins again.

In addition to approaching the book in this page-by-page format, you can experience the suggestions based focus points. Each focus point represents a personal life concern which you can access as necessary. If creating harmony is an issue in your life at present, reading the appropriate Feng Shui suggestions under the title Harmony will provide you with a means of action.

Additionally, the index organizes the material in *Wind and Water: Your Personal Feng Shui Journey* according to physical rooms or situations. For example, if you want further information about your home office, this listing will enable you to access that material.

I recommend that you first read the general information under the headings Feng Shui, Intention, and Bagua. These sections will provide you with the ground work for further reading. Near the end of the book is an exercise called Connecting to Your House that you can do continuously or little by little as you feel ready. I wish to acknowledge and thank Clare Cooper Marcus, author of *House As a Mirror of Self*, for the inspiration for this section.

Whether you use *Wind and Water: Your Personal Feng Shui Journey* as a daily exercise, a room-by-room guide, or a tool for dealing with personal concerns, you will be able to experience the flow of Feng Shui. As you begin to see changes manifest in your life, you will truly come to know what it means to create sacred space both inside and out. This is what Feng Shui is all about.

Feng Shui

Introduction

Feng Shui works with the circulation and flow of the life force (ch'i) in the living and working environment to create balance and harmony. It provides ways to create or select an ideal living or work-space to bring prosperity, productivity, and peace. Throughout the centuries, Feng Shui has been extensively used in all Eastern cultures. It has recently found its way to the West where it has gained popularity as people have come to realize its power.

Feng Shui gives a new perspective for viewing your life and the space where you live and work. It supports change. In many cases Feng Shui involves just plain common sense: if the faucet is leaking, call a plumber; if a light bulb is burned out, replace it; if a door sticks, fix it; if you want a new job, send out resumes and network. But in addition to these mundane changes, using the Feng Shui principle that "your space mirrors your life," you can begin to ask what besides the faucet was "leaking" out of your life, what else has "burned out" in your life, what issue is "sticky" for you right now. The Chinese have a poetic yet literal way of looking at issues. If you want to call something or someone into your life, use a bell or a chime. If you want to stop money from running out the front door, put an empty basket inside the door to catch the flow of wealth before it leaves your house. If you want some project or relationship to blossom, place a healthy, lush plant in the appropriate area to represent growth and vitality.

The adjustments for Feng Shui can be small and subtle and are usually affordable. An adjustment may not even be visible—a mirror placed in a closet or a business card tucked behind a picture can be as effective as re-arranging the entire living room furniture. The power of the adjustment does not depend on the object as much as the intention with which the object was placed. The stronger the intent, magnified by Feng Shui, the more dramatic the shifts that will manifest in your life.

Wind and Water: Your Personal Feng Shui Journey presents the subject in the format of simple suggestions that can be done on a daily basis. There are many other Feng Shui books that can provide the complete didactic text and approach. With this book, each page will provide some information about the theory or beliefs supporting Feng Shui and a corresponding activity. Instead of reading *about* Feng Shui, this book will provide an immediate experience of Feng Shui. The suggestions are appropriate to those who are novices to the subject as well as those who are familiar with its principles.

The intention of *Wind and Water: Your Personal Feng Shui Journey* is to demonstrate both the science and the art of this gentle Chinese art of place-ment. It is intended that you will gain a better understanding of what it is to incorporate Feng Shui into your space after seeing changes happen in your life. Your life will be influenced in some beautifully potent yet subtle ways by making mindful and intentional changes in your environment.

Everything is energy

During the course of the book you will be introduced to various Feng Shui principles and ideals. Each one is based on the fact that everything is energy and that your space reflects your life. As each day unfolds, you may feel yourself inspired to do some small gentle shift in your environment. You will find that as you do the small things, the larger things take care of themselves. Changing your environment does not have to be a daunting and forbidding task, but instead it can be an enjoyable process of dealing with one thing at a time.

Having a space with "good" Feng Shui doesn't mean that you won't have anything in it or that it will look like an Asian home. It doesn't mean you'll have to buy all new furniture or that the furniture you have doesn't meet the standards. "Good" Feng Shui definitely doesn't mean you have to use a certain kind of furniture or a certain color. And it doesn't mean you have to move. It does mean that you will have in your possession only those things which mean something to you. It means every room, every hallway, every closet, every cupboard will hold a special meaning for you. You will experience what it means to say, "I love my house."

Feng Shui is a process. As with your own growth mentally, emotionally, and spiritually, you will never be done. This is not meant to be discouraging but to make you aware that, as your life continues to change, so will your environment. Since your space reflects your life, it too will undergo some changes. Moving just one thing that hasn't been moved in at least six months can help you begin the Feng Shui journey. Anytime anything in your surroundings changes, so do you.

Love your living space

Feng Shui works on the principle that if you love your living space, you will be productive and creative. You only buy clothes in the style you like, in the size that fits, and in a color that's complimentary to your skin tone. When you wear clothes that you really love, you feel better and so you act better. Why is it that you will put things in your personal living space that not only don't you like but are not your style? As with a wardrobe, you need to be discerning and careful about what enters your front door. If you purchase a new sofa, then realize you don't like it, the sofa needs to be returned. If you inherit an antique armoire but you see it as being nothing more than an over-sized over-powering standing closet, then it needs to find another home. Having anything around that sets up negative feelings and makes you feel irritated, undermines your self-esteem. This will negatively affect your creativity, your productivity, and your financial income.

In Feng Shui it is important to look upon your home as a sanctuary. In a sanctuary you have only those things that make you feel unique, special and, above all, safe. If you cannot feel safe in your home, there's some disharmony that needs to be changed. Sometimes the disharmony comes from those who lived in the space prior to you. Often, what happened in the space before you moved in is not obvious, but a sense of uneasiness and discomfort on your part can point to some difficulties with your predecessors. Certainly if someone dies in the space, it's problematic for those living there later. Likewise, any abuse, even emotional abuse, can leave some negativity behind. But the most insidious can be when the negativity comes from unspoken thoughts and unexpressed anger. There's no evidence of violence but the potential was there nevertheless. All of these issues need to be cleared out before you can comfortably claim the space and make it into a sanctuary for your and your family.

Clear your space

When you clear a space, you claim it. Clearing a space means you clear out anything left over from the people who lived there before you. It can also mean clearing out some unpleasant incident that happened while you are currently living there—a verbal argument, a fight, a death in the house, any form of abuse. When you lift these negative events out of the space, claim it as your own. If you have just moved into a home or are about to, clearing it first is very effective and powerful. If you've lived in your space a while, you can still clear it with remarkable results. Many people can actually feel the difference after a clearing.

There are a number of ways to clear a space. The simplest is to walk through your space with incense, going into all the rooms, closets, cupboards, basement and attic, wafting the incense into all the areas. While doing this your intention is to not only clear any negativity, but also to bring blessings and good fortune into your life. You can clear a space with a candle, doing the same procedure. You can also use a bell, ringing it in all the rooms, cupboards, closets. Again, focus on the intention to clear and to bless. If you have none of these items, you could still walk through the house clapping your hands into all the areas.

In Feng Shui, the intention is to shift the energy in a space. If the energy has not been cleared first, the results of the Feng Shui adjustments can be unreliable. An analogy is like loading the dishwasher—sometimes you need to rinse the dishes first before putting them in the dishwasher to assure a cleaner job in the end. Make sure you've cleared your space before doing any of the Feng Shui suggestions. And from time to time you may find you'll want to do another clearing—maybe annually, after a party, after spring house cleaning or just because.

Feng Shui adjustments in layers

If a particular issue is very critical for you at this time in your life, you can layer your Feng Shui adjustments to give you optimum results. You layer your intention by working in the specific area in three different places in your home or office. For example, if money continues to be a serious concern for you, first locate the Wealth area in your home or apartment. In the back left corner place, with intention, something that represents money to you. This could take the form of a healthy plant if you're trying to grow a financial investment, a chime if you're trying to call in money in general, a fountain to signify the cash flow you're looking to bring in. Whatever you use, the adjustment needs to be appropriately suited to your taste and to engage your intention so as to remind you of what you're asking for.

Secondly, locate the Wealth area of your bedroom and make an appropriate change in the environment there as well. It does not have to be the same object that was used in the first area. In the bedroom you may want to bring in something purple or lavender since this is the color that represents money—an amethyst or a lavender candle. If you don't want to use your bedroom to make an adjustment, use another room in your house.

Third, to add another layer to your wealth intention, do something appropriate on your desk in the Wealth corner. A bell, some flowers, a $100 bill under a statue—anything you use will support and enhance the adjustments you've made in the other parts of your house. It is suggested you use this layered approach when an issue is having a serious impact on your life or when you want results within a quick timeframe.

The Yin-Yang theory of change

One of the principles Feng Shui is based upon is the Yin/Yang theory of continual change. The circular Yin/Yang symbol represents ever-constant, ever-changing activity. Any circular or oval shapes used throughout your space represent movement, balance, and flow.

The round Yin/Yang symbol exemplifies the cycle of flow from one extreme to its opposite. The black area moves from the least amount to the fullest at the same time the white area is moving from its fullest to its least. Yet within the area where there's the most white, there's a small amount of black beginning to seed. In the area where the black is the fullest, you can see a small amount of white beginning to grow. This interprets into the principle that if you're very, very happy there's a small amount of sadness beginning to grow; likewise if you're very, very sad there's happiness soon to come. Nothing stays the same. Everything cycles.

The Yin/Yang symbol is representative of the flow of nature where seasons come and go and cycles swing from one to another. Despite your best efforts you cannot stop this cycle—it continues its movement no matter what. By flowing with these cycles they become less difficult and you can exemplify the peace and harmony intended for everyone to experience.

Enjoy every space in your home

Each room of your house, each closet, each hallway, everywhere you sit needs to be regarded as a pleasant "event." This means that each and every square inch of your space is to be regarded with the same respect as your living room or your bedroom. It doesn't matter if it's the back hall closet or a hallway that simply moves you through the house. You want to enjoy going from one room to the other, or from one end of the house to the other, or from one floor to another.

If there's a room or a closet you absolutely despise or, at best, can only tolerate, that should be a red flag for you. What can you do to change that feeling? Cleaning it out may be appropriate. Painting may be necessary. Rearranging the furniture may be all that's required. Even the smallest, most unused closet is part of your house. Ignoring any spaces in your house is bad luck—it's a metaphor for ignoring something in your own life.

You may be surprised to find that the least favorite spot or room can become the one area you gravitate toward once you've initiated some changes. A grungy old back hall becomes a delight to walk into once it's cleaned and painted. Removing old winter coats that aren't worn anymore makes a crowded front closet usable and workable again so that hanging up jackets and putting away scarves isn't a tiresome chore. Painting a hallway a fun, exciting color gives a whole new meaning to walking upstairs. Utilizing all your space to the fullest brings with it not only room you didn't know you had, but also energy you didn't know existed within your walls.

Your home is your version of the world

Without leaving your home, you can begin to comprehend the rest of the world. In setting up or selecting your surroundings, you create, knowingly or unknowingly, a microcosm of your version of the world. Your perspective of life is filtered through your environment. If you change your environment you change your perspective. If you have to filter through a lot of baggage to see what's happening, you cannot see clearly. Your world becomes heavy and does not allow you to fly free.

You can begin to comprehend not only how the universe works but also how to finesse it, how to work with it, how to love it. As you finesse/work/love your own environment, it automatically translates to the bigger mirror of the outer world. The control you exert over the physical space that you agreed to caretake enables you to better control the outer elements of your life. There is no skipping this part. If you can't manage your affairs at home, there will be less chance of you managing them elsewhere.

As the intensity of life increases daily and appears to be spinning out of control, it is more and more important that you hold and anchor some control in your own personal world. You cannot control the world, but you can control your home. Allowing a space to impact you negatively, to throw up your hands in despair at the mess, to walk through piles of challenges without dealing with them, is a clear and direct invitation for the entire world to mirror back to you the life you have created. Be mindful of your reflection outward.

"As inner, so outer"

If you understand the maxim "as inner, so outer," you can begin to understand the impact you can have without leaving your home. It explains and justifies the lifestyle of cloistered monks who seemingly don't contribute anything outward to the community—yet their impact upon the lives of people they have never met cannot be overlooked. These monks have their own inner world in order, radiating it out to others. Likewise, as you get your own inner world in order, the effects will be felt beyond your capacity to imagine.

Changing your message to the universe is done in small steps, despite the enormity of the task at first glance. You clean a drawer, you straighten up a room, you paint a wall. Your universe is changing and so is your message, so is your mirror to others. As you make these small baby-step changes, you not only refine what you broadcast out to others, but more importantly you refine what you're broadcasting to yourself. The universe is really inside you. Through the assistance of your spatial environment you can come to know yourself.

"As inner, so outer" refers not only to the comparison of your home to the outside world, but also refers to the comparison of the inner you to your home. Changing one affects the other. Sometimes changing the outer to affect and support changes from the inside is appropriate. Sometimes changing the inner radiates changes on the outer world. Sometimes you need changes coming from both directions.

An act of faith

When making Feng Shui adjustments with clarity and intention, it is important to explore whether the adjustments originate from a need to make a change or whether they express a change that has already been accomplished. Often people will buy a new car to celebrate a career move, or they will proceed with a remodeling project after a raise. If you are a newly divorced person you may paint the bedroom after your partner has finally agreed to sign divorce papers or you may buy a new bedroom set to celebrate your new-found freedom and the end to an unhappy journey.

On the other hand, making the adjustments ahead of time to elicit the changes you want is an act of faith. What if you buy that new car before the job was offered to you? What if you didn't wait for the raise to do a much needed remodeling project? What if your bedroom was re-painted and furnished with new items before the final decree? These adjustments can assist and enhance what you're hoping and dreaming for if done with trust and clarity. They can bring about changes far surpassing your expectations. As you have changed your inner, smaller world to reflect what you wanted—the outer world will follow suit. And you have done it with trust.

This approach doesn't condone spending crazily and carelessly in anticipation of a new job or a raise. It does however require that you are clear about what you want and that you have a clarity and insight into realistic anticipations. It requires that you not live in fear but instead you live with assurance that your needs will be met. If buying a car before the raise seems negligent and presumptuous, then you must listen to your inner voice. But there's a possibility that buying the car before the raise is the only way you'll get the raise!

Linking the inner and outer worlds

Creating a direct link between the inner world and the outer world is the power that Feng Shui provides. If you cannot find peace in your home because there's nowhere you can go to be peaceful or because there's unfinished business all over, clutter stacked up in piles and invasive noise, then you won't be able to deal very well with the battles going on inside. On inner levels you will also be dealing with unfinished business, clutter in the form of too many activities and too many people making demands, and noise from the unceasing chatter going on in your mind. Likewise, the world outside your home will not be comforting since your mirror will extend those feelings out into the bigger world.

You can take meditation classes to begin to quiet your mind and thoughts, but you can also remove the clutter in your physical space. You can resolve a relationship that needs to end just as you can finish painting the hallway—a project that started many months ago. Whichever one of these activities begins first doesn't matter—they each reflect the other. Sometimes they begin simultaneously. Or you may simply decide to finish the hallway project this coming weekend, when out of the blue the person involved in your dubious relationship comes calling, wanting to resolve the unresolved.

The outer world will become a better, less frightening place when you've dealt with your own demons first. The support from your living space, as it reflects back to you what changes you've made on the inside, helps you confront and face what is waiting for you in the outer world. Then, your life mirror is a peaceful reflection that radiates that comfort outward and reflects it back into your life.

The longing to "go home"

Deep in the heart of each and every person there's a secret longing to "go home." This may not, and usually doesn't, mean the home where you were raised as a child. Due to difficult circumstances, dysfunctional family situations and unpleasant memories, you may never want to return to that house. Yet people ache to "go home." They just don't know where that is.

"Finding home" is an unending process. However, you can get very, very close to "being home." You may experience being home for a while in a certain place and time in your life, but then things change. You change. Your family changes and your needs change. The search for home starts again. Finding home is all about finding safety and security, unquestioning love and compassion. Finding home is far more than a house or an apartment, but that's a good place to begin. If you can be home in your physical space, finding home in your emotional, mental, and spiritual space is a lot easier.

If your physical home holds no interest for you because it reminds you of sad, violent, or desperate times, it is difficult to feel at home there but not impossible. Or, if your physical home annoys and frustrates you with the upkeep and maintenance, it is difficult to feel at home there. The two options in both these cases are to move or to find a way to make it a home for yourself. If you opt for the latter, select one corner, one chair, or one room and set up a base camp for yourself. Arrange it with your favorite things. Make it known to other people who live with you that this is your area alone and nothing is to be touched except by you. Remember, "Home is where the heart is." Put your heart into this little spot. Once you've got it just the way you want it, once you can experience the splendor of your own special place, and once you sense its safety for you, no matter what has happened during your day, you can always "come home."

Intention

Energy is the common bond

One of the scientific principles upon which Feng Shui is based is that everything is energy. All things in the universe are connected by a common bond—you, a flower, a river, a tree, a book, your house. Everything connects and is related to everything else by this bond. The difference between you and your house, for instance, is simply the make-up of the energy. As humans you have the added advantage of being aware of this phenomenon and of being able to alter this energy with your thoughts and intentions.

Each object that you own connects to you and requires your attention. You need to either move it, clean it, store it, water it, dust it, or provide whatever care it needs. When you have a lot of objects around you, your energy gets diffused as it is spread out over many, many items. Then you begin to not "see" what you have. You can walk by a picture time and time again without really looking at it; you no longer notice the specially mixed paint color you used on your bedroom walls; you take for granted the beautiful crystal you hung in the window. You no longer consciously connect with what you own.

Living with intention requires that your eyes be open and that they be discerning. By looking at what you own and making a clear decision about whether this enhances or depletes your energy, you can begin to experience the flow of Feng Shui. Your environment needs to speak of your intention in order for you to make the changes you want in your life. Each object you own and have in your space needs to also be in harmony with this intention. The discernment comes from knowing what objects are drawing energy from you and whether you can expend the energy it takes to keep or not keep something.

You "tame" what you own

Whatever you own, you "tame" according to *The Little Prince* by Antoine de Saint-Exupery. When you take something into your life, it becomes yours and it becomes unique. There may be a thousand others like it somewhere in the world, but the one you have is special because you have allowed a bond to happen. When a bond happens, there's a connection of energy and then there's some responsibility.

Owning things can become quite awesome when you begin to own a lot of things. They all require energy and time at some point. If you're not willing to give that, the object becomes a negative drain and it's time to get rid of it. Just as with close friends, you can only manage a certain number before it becomes hard to juggle your social calendar—everyone wants a piece of your time and energy. You consciously or unconsciously begin to discern with whom you'll spend time, slowly eliminating those who, for whatever reason, no longer fit in your life. As you take stock of what you own, you need to ask whether you want to take the time required to "tame" it. You have only so much energy to go around and so, as with friends, you need to decide what is most important. Honesty with yourself and clarity about your intention will make this process happen. Each object you have in your space must enhance your life, must promote your creativity, and must make you feel like the special, unique individual that you are. Otherwise, it doesn't belong in your sanctuary.

Turn intention into physical representation

As you begin to understand and experience the common bond between yourself and everything you own, you will tap into additional sources of energy to bring about the changes you want in life. When you're invested in something, whether it's an original painting, a handmade candle, a shell from a beach in Mexico, or a beautiful shade of lavender painted on your bedroom walls, you've established an energetic bond. Each time you look at the painting, the candle, the shell, the walls, etc., you re-connect with the experience. The object holds that experience for you so that all you have to do is see it and you're instantly re-connected to the feelings of exhilaration, delight, inner peace, or whatever you first experienced with it.

By the power of your thoughts and of your attention, you enable that object to hold an intention on your behalf. You already love the object so why not assign it a "mission" to bring in or enhance what you want in your life. Your thoughts are energy which you can infuse into any object to hold the focus for you. Magnifying your intention this way helps to "up the odds" so that what you want will come about.

The power of Feng Shui comes from "programming" your intention into a physical representation. This physical object acts as a reminder to you of what your focus is lest you forget. It only takes one object to magnify your intention—not ten or fifty. Having four amethyst stones where one will suffice begins to speak of mistrust of the power of the energy. One item will work fine. Remember, it's your intention that strengthens the focus of the object not the number of objects.

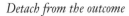

Detach from the outcome

Setting an intention in an object requires blind faith in the Universe. You must believe that it hears your request, understands what you want, and provides what you need. There will be no confirmation letters or faxes; you can only trust that things will come about as they should. A very important ingredient in setting an intention is the ability to detach from the outcome. You will need to let go of how it will happen. Getting bound up in the details of how and when things will manifest is at cross purposes to your belief that everything is connected. There is a wisdom in Nature and in the Universe that will bring you what you ask for or something even better, but only when you let go of the control.

Your only job in this process is to "laser" in on what your dreams are and set the intention in an object or activity. Get clear about what you want in your life. You can write down a "wish list" if it helps and then select one for the moment. Then incorporate that intention or wish into some physical representation. Even the activity of cleaning a closet can be intentional. The delight in seeing the results of those efforts can be a powerful boost to your intention. It is important not to obsess over how your wish is going to happen. If you request for more money to flow into your life, you do not want to dilute your focus by questioning how this could possibly occur. Be aware of and change your ongoing limiting thoughts: "I have a fixed income. How would I ever get more money? It's silly to ask for more money because it wouldn't ever happen." With this kind of sentiment added to your intention, it won't happen. Let go of how the channels will open to bring you what you asked for. You need only believe that it will occur.

Prioritize the changes you want

When first starting to do Feng Shui in your life, it is important that you prioritize the changes you want to bring about. If you have many issues that need attention at this time in your life, spend a few moments picking the top three that are most critical. If you try to do too much at once, your energy will be scattered and you could be inviting too much activity into your life at a time when that might be the opposite of your goal.

Once you've decided on the top three issues, begin with the first one and make three adjustments that seem appropriate. For example, if money is your main concern right now, you might want to clean out a cluttered closet in the money area of your house. In addition, you might want to bring a fresh, healthy plant into the Wealth area of your bedroom to represent growth. Finally, you may want to place a bank on your desk in the Wealth area or a bell to call in additional funds. After these three items are in place and you've been clear about your intention, let go of the outcome. Let the items begin to call in what you want. If you're continually fussing over results that aren't happening fast enough or results that are coming in differently than expected, you're at cross purposes with the natural flow of events.

Those three items will have their intention reinforced each and every time you look at them, clean them, water them, ring them, move them. Doing anything further is your blatant statement that you're sure either the Universe hasn't heard your request or you don't trust that the items already in place know what to do. If any doubt or misgiving is allowed, you've undermined your intentions and they, indeed, will not work.

Simplify your life

Feng Shui is about simplifying your life. If you feel overwhelmed when thinking about doing adjustments for Feng Shui, then you are elaborating the process and making it much more complicated than it should be. It doesn't mean you have to take valuable, precious hours out of an already overcrowded schedule in order to do some Feng Shui. But it does mean you have to spend a few moments centering yourself long enough to know what needs changing or enhancing.

The changes and shifts in your space do not have to be drastic. One adjustment, one crystal, one shelf that has been cleared off is just as effective as rearranging your whole living room. To quote the architect Mies van der Rohe, "Less is more." Feng Shui is not about creating more projects, nor is it about leaving less time in your day. It is about helping to make your life easier, richer, and more satisfying.

Nor is Feng Shui about bringing more things into your life just when you've been purging old items. Hanging crystals and windchimes, installing an aquarium, bringing in a fountain—all of these things if done to excess can begin another sort of clutter. Be mindful of how many things you use. Your intention clearly focused on one object can bring about as many changes as someone who puts in three things in the same area. In fact, the results will be clearer and more direct with one object. If a cookie recipe calls for a cup of sugar, but just to make sure you decide to add a little honey and some brown sugar, the end result will be different than if you had stuck to the original ingredient. The cookies won't be as good either.

Perceiving the results

There are times when it may seem to you that Feng Shui isn't working. There don't seem to be any results. You may begin to wonder if you did the right adjustment, or if you should do something more or change it altogether. Because many of the adjustments begin on very subtle energy levels, it is difficult to say when obvious shifts in a situation can be expected. Results can come within hours of doing a Feng Shui alignment or it may take months to realize your intention. Most of this depends upon whether or not a change is ready to surface. Feng Shui can hasten the process. But if a major adjustment is required, there are times when it may seem to take longer than expected.

Sometimes you have an ability to adapt to the worst situations and so you may ignore certain things in the environment. For instance, if one of your intentions is to get a pay-raise at work, yet you are involved in an abusive relationship at home, any intentions around the increase in pay cannot work as well. Feng Shui is about creating balance and harmony. When there's obvious imbalance in one aspect of your life, you will find it difficult to achieve what you want in another aspect. By ignoring the abuse at home, your intentions at work are undermined. It would seem on the outside that Feng Shui is not working when you get overlooked for that raise. Yet if you're not worthy of considerate treatment at home, then you're not worthy of considerate and fair treatment at work. Your intention needs to be more focused on general, overall balance in all aspects of your life.

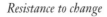

Resistance to change

Despite doing Feng Shui adjustments to facilitate some change in your life, there is always a natural resistance to things changing. You may even find it hard to leave or change difficult situations because there's a tendency to leave things as they are. If an adjustment is made in any area while harboring a strong subconscious objection to making any changes, Feng Shui won't work.

If, by hanging a windchime outside your front door, you are trying to call in a new job with better pay and new opportunities, yet all the while you're seriously questioning your qualifications for this new position, Feng Shui will probably not work. If you're dreading the move to a new job because it will require driving further to get to work, a new wardrobe, longer hours, or more travel, again Feng Shui is being sabotaged. If it's simply that your best friend works at the old job and you know how much you'll miss being together and how sad you're going to feel, how you're going to miss your lunches together, your coffee breaks, the rides homes, etc., etc., Feng Shui doesn't have your full commitment. Making any adjustments for your career will be difficult since it is only your words that have made the commitment, not your heart.

Being ready to receive

A Feng Shui adjustment may not work when you are not ready to receive it. If the adjustment representing what you're trying to manifest doesn't seem to be bringing results, it may be in your best interest. You may be trying to sell your house for six months because you have a contingency offer on the "house of your dreams." Without the sale of your current home, you can't afford to proceed with the purchase of the other home. Much to your frustration, and despite many Feng Shui adjustments in the Helpful People area of your current home, it never sells. Later, you may find that the "house of your dreams" had structural problems costing the new owners thousands of dollars. Furthermore, you may also discover that another house comes along that is even better for you than the one you thought was already perfect— and for less money! Things happen in their own time.

In hindsight, it's obvious that the Feng Shui adjustment was working very well—in fact, better than you thought or imagined! Yet while enduring the disappointments of losing one home and not selling another, it is easy to lose sight of the fact that there is a bigger picture and one in which you will get more than you bargained for. When delays in getting a new job, or getting a book published, or clinching a business deal approach high levels of exasperation, keep in mind that your intention has set things in motion and it will unfold in the appropriate time.

Some results are gentle

The results of a Feng Shui adjustment are often discounted because they are not recognized. The results are either very subtle and gentle or the change very different than what was expected. In either case, the Feng Shui adjustment did support your intention—you were simply looking for something else.

Asking for a new job, and making Feng Shui adjustments accordingly, may come in the form of a promotion in the same job. Or it may mean a new job description in which your duties are different but you still have the same desk and the same pay. Or it may mean a new love interest has begun working at your place of business and suddenly you find yourself anxious to go to work! In your expectation of having a job at a new company, you may not see that your current job has taken on new meaning.

Likewise, asking for additional money in your life may not always mean that a lottery check shows up in the mail. Your car insurance may drop, you may get an unexpected rebate on a new car, you may find a bank error in your favor, or you may find a buyer for your old piano. All of these situations indicate an increase in money, even though it may not be packaged as you thought. Doing Feng Shui requires being mindful and sensitive to what comes your way and recognizing everything it brings into your life.

Bagua

The bagua

In Feng Shui, the bagua is a mental tool or map that is used to determine the placement of nine life issues as they are represented in your space. Feng Shui is based on a principle that your space reflects your life. When a bagua is appropriately placed and enhanced, your life begins to manifest good fortune and blessed occurrences. The nine areas are laid out as shown below.

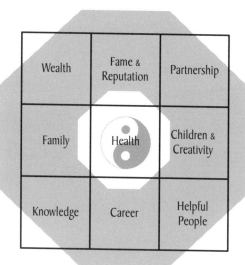

This mental map can be placed over the main floor of a building or a home, an individual room, or even a desk top. The orientation of the bagua is determined by the position of the front door. The front door may not be the door you use all of the time. Nevertheless, the entrance that was architecturally intended to be the front door is the one with which you will work. The front entrance will always be in the Knowledge, Career, or Helpful People area.

If you look at your space as though flying above it, include in the bagua anything that has a roof and sides. Therefore, include an attached garage in the bagua. A screened-in porch is also part of the layout. A deck and overhangs will not be part of the layout since they do not have both a roof and sides.

After incorporating all the pieces that need to be included, divide your space into three equal areas left to right and three equal areas front to back. Each area matches one of those shown on the bagua drawing. Now you can see that, if, from the perspective of the street, your front door is to the left on the house, you have a Knowledge door. If your front door is in the center, you have a Career door. Likewise, if your door is located more to the right, you have a Helpful People door.

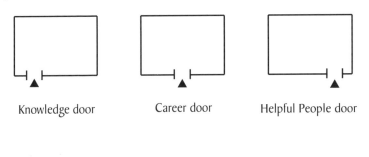

Knowledge door   Career door   Helpful People door

As you first begin to lay out the bagua, do not concern yourself with the interior walls. Be most concerned with mapping out the different bagua areas on the overall layout. However, once you have located the nine areas, you can locate the different rooms in relation to the bagua. The Wealth area is in the back, left corner of your space. The Partnership area is in the back, right corner. The Health area is in the center, etc.

You will probably realize that your house is not a perfect square or rectangle. In all likelihood, it will have some pieces protruding and some cutting into the space. When a piece is missing, it indicates a depletion or challenge in that bagua area. You want to "capture" missing areas by planting a tree in the corner, installing a flagpole, or a light post, running a fence around the area, putting in a fountain or birdbath, or creating any marker that will reinforce your intention to complete what is missing.

missing piece in Partnership

missing piece in Career

If you have little pieces protruding from the main part of your house, you have an extension in the corresponding area of the bagua. An extension is auspicious and gives you extra energy in that particular area. Extensions do not need to be changed.

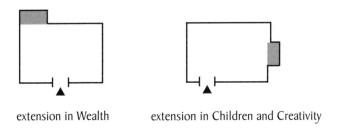

extension in Wealth   extension in Children and Creativity

There are times when it is difficult to determine which way the bagua lays out. For example, you might have a hidden or slanted door. Then you incorporate the Feng Shui bagua on a room-by-room basis. When you lay out a bagua over an individual room, determine the front entry to the room. If you have more than one entry, the front is the one used most frequently. Most often, the bagua areas of an individual room are in a different orientation than the bagua of the whole house or building. It is not important that they match.

Many layers

By having many layers of the bagua with which to work (your house, a room, a desk, your bed), you can elicit changes from different facets of your life. You can choose only those areas that reflect things you want to change in your life. If health is currently a problem, go to the Health area of your whole space, and/or the Health area in a specific room (the bedroom, for example), and/or the Health area on your desk to enhance your health. If you are in a serious health situation, you may want to change something in all three areas. If health is not an issue in your life right now, there is no need to make changes in those areas.

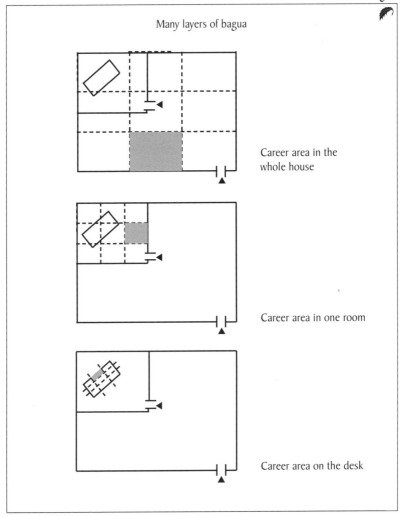

Many layers of bagua

Career area in the whole house

Career area in one room

Career area on the desk

Bagua

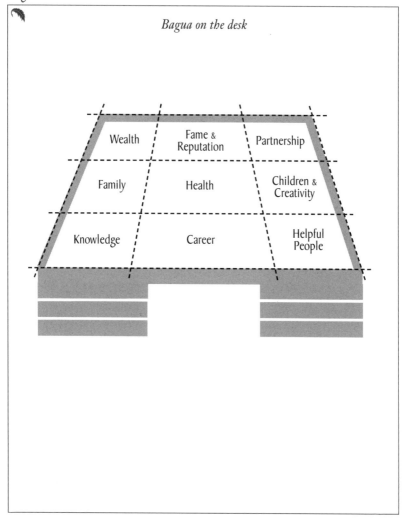

Bagua on the desk

Wealth	Fame & Reputation	Partnership
Family	Health	Children & Creativity
Knowledge	Career	Helpful People

Bagua on the bed

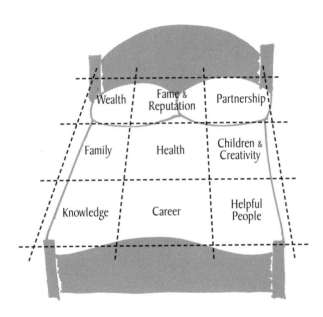

More in-depth information on each of the nine bagua areas follows the sections on Colors, Elements, and Trigrams.

Colors

Each area of the bagua (Knowledge, Family, Wealth, etc.) is represented by a specific color. The color, or its variation, can be used in the corresponding part of the bagua. If Wealth is currently a problematic situation, you can integrate something purple, lavender, magenta, or mauve in that area. Since colors are so personal, it is very important that you use a color and a shade or tone that you love.

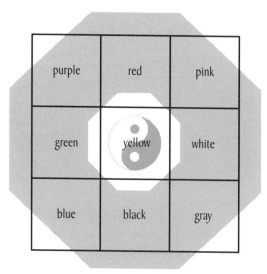

Elements

Each area of the bagua is represented by a corresponding element from nature such as mountain, thunder, wind, etc. These elements provide further insight into how to work with each area and how to understand them on another level. The words used to describe the elements are strictly metaphorical, although literal images can be effectively employed in using them.

Trigrams

Each area of the bagua is also represented by a trigram which is comprised of a specific order of three positive (Yang) and/or negative (Yin) lines. The positive lines are straight across; the negative lines have a break. By knowing the trigram for each area, you can utilize its symbol as a means of making or assisting some changes in a particular part of your life.

The use of the trigrams in making changes in your life takes your intention to a more subtle level. Whenever something gets more subtle, it gets more powerful. There is a refinement in your intention that takes on a whole new dimension. If you listen to an opera in its original language, it almost always will be more impactful than listening to a translation of the dialogue, even if you don't understand the original language. The trigrams are like the original language of the bagua.

Career

A career is a direction to utilize your abilities, talents, and interests. A career takes you from one phase of your life to the next. It is a vehicle for your passion, even if you don't get paid for it. Many people find enjoyment in their paying professions, yet they also love to volunteer, garden, sky dive, and paint. All of these are activities and directions for your pursuits and are classified under the Career area of the bagua.

The element for Career is the river, which speaks to a journey or path. A river takes you through time and space as do your interests and hobbies. If your career is a particular issue right now, you can use the image of the river to help adjust the situation. Hanging a picture of a river in the Career area of your home or your bedroom will remind you of your journey. The river image flows gently, making subtle but persistent changes along the way.

The river trigram is made up of two broken lines, one on top and one on the bottom, with a solid line in the middle. The receptivity of the earth on either side of the river provides a pictogram of the river element. Placing a copy of the river trigram in the Career area of your desk (maybe under a piece of glass that covers the top of your desk) can be effective. You can also tuck it between the mattress and box spring of your bed in the Career area (at the foot of the bed). You can also carry a copy of it in your pocket when the intensity of this issue begins to increase (i.e., asking for a raise, making a sales pitch to a critical client, vying for a promotion).

Knowledge

The area of Knowledge is about learning and education in whatever form that may take for you—a high school diploma, a graduate degree, a certification or license in a field that calls you. It can also be about your children's educational issues. It further reflects the ascent to higher self-knowledge; in other words, learning about yourself. It also reflects the undertaking to share your knowledge or information.

Whether true or not, it is a perception that holy men and women live on top of the mountain—closer to heaven, a shorter distance to access higher knowledge and insight. Hence, the Knowledge area is represented by the mountain. Whether knowledge is more internally based or externally oriented, it usually requires some contemplation and climbing toward the end result. Placing a picture or poster of a mountain in the Knowledge area can reflect the climb to new information.

The trigram is comprised of two broken lines on the bottom and one solid line across the top. The mountain trigram depicts the receptive energy of the earth with a pinnacle across the top. It is reminiscent of the stones at Stonehenge with two pillars supporting a horizontal cap. Incorporating the trigram representation of the mountain/Knowledge area can be an effective way to bring about some changes. Using a copy of the trigram printed on a piece of paper as a bookmark in a course of studies may bring some interesting insights. Having a copy of the trigram in your hands or on your altar while meditating can assist your ascent to new heights.

Family

Family issues include your family of origin such as parents, siblings, cousins, and relations. It also includes anyone you consider your extended family such as good friends, neighbors, and colleagues. This area is most commonly recognized as dealing with your roots and where you came from. It also reflects any groups brought together for a specific purpose, such as work teams, book clubs, ski groups, and fundraising committees.

Thunder is the element associated with the Family area of the bagua. Thunder can bring sparks and shifts in a dramatic way. The dynamics are similar to those found in many families of origin or any group of people dedicated to a special project. There may indeed be sparks of creativity, opposition, and accomplishment in these group dynamics. Many times thunder will clear the air for moving ahead. Anything that reminds you of thunder can be appropriate in the Family area. Pictures of lighting, or the zig-zag shape itself in a painting or fabric can assist in easing family tensions, assuring success in a group endeavor, or maintaining cohesiveness in a business association.

The thunder trigram is depicted with one solid line on the bottom with two broken lines stacked above it. If you can see the image of the thunderbolts coming down from the heavens in the trigram, you can sense the connection of the thunder to the land below. The land is looking upward to meet the thunder. There's an upward orientation and a vital life force with thunder. A copy of the Thunder trigram can be folded up and placed under a vase of flowers in the middle of a conference table or dinner table to bring about some harmony during a difficult confrontation.

Wealth

Wealth is about your money, both coming in and going out. How you get your money (wages, lottery, inheritance, stocks, funding, gifts) balances how you spend your money (expenses, gifts, charity, inheritance, retirement).

The Wealth area is associated with the element of wind. Just as your money needs to flow and move, so does the wind. A common tendency is to hang onto wealth that comes in or has accumulated; yet, the element of wind clearly suggests that letting it come and go is the correct balance. A gentle breeze comes and goes. When the breeze is stagnant and not seeming to move very much, a person can feel almost suffocated from the stale air. On a hot still day, there's nothing like a fresh breeze to revitalize your outlook on life. When money has been tight, it's very refreshing to land a "windfall," immensely changing your outlook. Watching too much wind destroying trees and buildings can cause panic. Likewise, when money flows out in excessive amounts, you can only watch in helplessness as you rearrange your life to accommodate expenses. Achieve as much balance as you can with the wind element.

The wind trigram is represented by a broken line on the bottom with two solid lines stacked on top. The visual message is movement over the land or earth. The two solid lines represent the air or wind blowing across the base of the land. If one of the solid lines is going in one direction and the other going in the opposite direction, you have a budgetary plan for your own income and outflow of wealth.

Fame and Reputation

The Fame and Reputation area stands for your image and how the world sees you. It represents your good name and your standing in the community. In a business setting, it reflects your connection to the outside, and becoming known for what you do.

Fire is the element that can make you known. With too much fire, everyone may know you, not because you're famous, but because you've become infamous. With too little fire, no one will know who you are. The core of fire is reflective of focus, purpose, and direction. You may have a plan or an idea but, without the spark or flame required to put it into action, nothing much may happen. Too much fire can cause "burnout." A fire in balance will bring you the clarity you're searching for around a particular issue. It can let your name get out in the world appropriately, and it can move your project along on its path. Any new business endeavor needs to have its fire in balance to get up and running. Using a candle can set the stage for your enlightenment. Every time you light the candle, you hold and reinforce your intention.

The fire trigram is composed of a broken line in the center with a sold line on the top and a solid line on the bottom. As with the heart of a flame, the trigram depicts the center core. A copy of the fire trigram can be placed in the Fame and Reputation area of your desk or in the Fame and Reputation area of your office behind a picture.

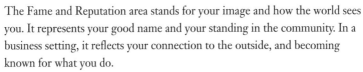

Partnership

The Partnership area reflects personal partners, business partners, spiritual partners, and partnering with yourself. Getting to know yourself or working through some issues with a partner fall into this category.

The Partnership area is represented by the earth element. This element stands for stability and anchoring. If you have earth in balance, your partnerships will be solid yet allow you the individual freedom to expand. If the earth is out of balance, you can feel mired down by the heaviness of certain relationships. Using stones, sand altars, pictures of the earth, or clay pots, you can affect the partnerships in your life. Placing two stones or crystals in the Partnership area of your bedroom represents your intention for a solid and secure relationship between you and your partner. Placing two green plants in clay pots on your desk can assist in easing any business partnership tension.

The earth trigram is three broken lines stacked one on top of the other. This speaks to the receptivity and openness of the earth element. The trigram doesn't speak to action as much as it does to stability. For example, a copy of the trigram can be placed between the mattress and box spring of your bed in the Partnership area, keeping in mind that you want to call in a suitable partner and be a suitable partner as well.

Children and Creativity

Children and Creativity stands for your own children, other children you may be involved with, and your inner child. It also includes all things for which you will be remembered—a book, a thesis, your stories, your music.

The lake is the element associated with this area. When you work with your creative energy, you are, in effect, dipping into the pool of imagination and inspiration to bring forth your legacy. A picture of a lake in the Children and Creativity area of your studio or your home will enhance your creative effort. A pond in the Children and Creativity area of your lot could remind you of the reflection required to birth your creations. Placing pictures of children or pictures of you as a child in your Children and Creativity area can significantly manifest playful, free, and imaginative undertakings. Special toys or a doll can plant some fertile seeds as well.

The lake trigram is comprised of two solid lines on the bottom with one broken line on the top. Just as earth forms a hollow for water to fill in, the trigram shows the top earth line forming a hollow for the lake underneath. Sleeping with a copy of the lake trigram in the Children and Creativity area of your bed between the mattress and box spring can bring you visions of inspiration.

Helpful People

Helpful people are often referred to as "angels," particularly when they show up unexpectedly with exactly what you need when you need it. Helpful people are those who support you emotionally and sometimes financially. They can be a best friend, a relative, a minister, a plumber. A helpful person can be a realtor who helps you sell your house or a travel agent who gets you from here to there. A helpful person can be a client for your business. As part of the ebb and flow of Feng Shui, being a helpful person is as important as having helpful people or benefactors in your life. Sometimes you need to be one before you will see any benefactors manifest in your own life.

Appropriately, the element for Helpful People is heaven. What better place from which to encounter angels. If you want more helpful people in your life, use the heaven element by placing a picture or a painting of heavenly scenes, pictures of angels, or any power symbols that are important to you. Placing them in the Helpful People area of your home or office will tap into their strongest power. The heaven element is sometimes referred to as the sky element, so you can also use anything that speaks to you of sky.

The trigram for heaven is three stacked solid lines. It represents nature at its fullest and most active. It is the position of command and power. Using this trigram in the Helpful People area of your home or bedroom can bring in the "angels" you're looking for.

Health

The center of the bagua is the Health area. This area represents health on physical, mental, emotional and spiritual levels. By placing Health in the center, a hub or core is created around which everything else revolves. It follows that if you are not feeling well, you do not do your job well; you do not relate to your partner or your children in a patient, loving manner; your productivity and creativity are affected; your pay may even be affected. Feeling well is crucial to functioning well.

When you're feeling scattered or unfocused, something in the Health area is unbalanced. Depression, fatigue, eating disorders, allergies—these are all reflected in the center of your space. Keeping the center harmonious, balanced and honored is a crucial step in your life's journey.

The Health area does not have a specific element of nature since it represents nature in its entirety. It also has no trigram but is represented by the tai ch'i or Yin-Yang symbol which represents all of life in its ebb and flow. Placing the tai ch'i symbol in the center of your home or your bedroom can dramatically represent your intention for health. Wearing this symbol as a pendant or necklace can be a powerful experience to connect you with your "wind" and "water."

Inner Strength

Command position

It's hard to know which comes first: if you're in control of your life it follows that you will have control of your space, or whether once you have control of your space, your life will fall into place. Usually people who have control over their own personal living space know where their lives are headed or at least have a general direction. To assist in capturing and sustaining this sense of power, there are command positions in Feng Shui based on where your front door is located. Any command position is located in the back corner of a space at the greatest angle from the front door. If, when standing outside your house, your front door is on the right-hand side of the space, your command position is in the back left corner. Likewise, if, when looking at your house from the outside, your front door is on the left-hand side then your command position is in the back right corner.

If your front door is in the center of your space as you observe it from its outside perspective, then you have two command positions—one in the back left corner and one in the back right corner. Some people will have their command position in the garage, others in the kitchen or a bedroom. Knowing where your command positions are, you can tap into their power to help you call in what you want in your life. A command position assists you in establishing your identity in the space. It can help to solidify your mission of stewardship of the land and the property. As the owner of the space, it is important that you utilize the command position of your house or apartment.

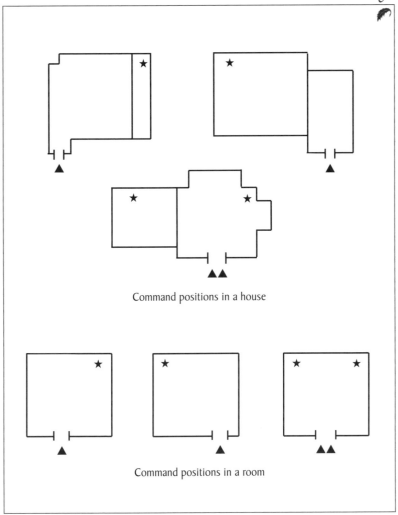

Command positions in a house

Command positions in a room

Occupying the command position

It is ideal to have your bedroom in a command position of your home if you are the principle owner of the space. Because it establishes ownership and control, you would not want your children's bedrooms in the command position for they will certainly run your life. You would not want a guest room in this position for guests will never want to leave. Command positions are by nature very inviting. People gravitate toward these corners because they feel so comforting.

It is advisable to move your child or any children who are occupying a command position in your house. Trade rooms with them if necessary even if it requires a slight down-size in scale. If you don't want the smaller room, at least try to find another place for your child. Then you can occupy the old bedroom as your own office or reading room. It is fine if the kitchen or dining room is taking command. And it's not problematic if the family room is located there. If you have a home office located in the command position, be mindful of not having your work take over your life.

There's always a possibility that the command position can end up in the back corner of an attached garage. As with any command post, you need to keep things in order. Garages tend to accumulate "stuff" often without any awareness on your part—it just happens. Although you never want unidentified objects (flying or otherwise) to congregate in your space, you particularly don't want them in your command position. This situation will undermine your authority and your control over your space (life).

Maintaining your command

If a child is occupying a command position in your home and there are no other rooms for them to move into, you can establish your presence in this area in other ways. One way is to have a picture of yourself in the child's room so that your identity is physically seen in that space. If not a picture, then something else that is definitely from you—some artwork you have done, a quilt you may have made, furniture you have built for the room, etc. If there's nothing of you taking command in this room, then it is only natural for the person occupying the space to assume the control.

If, on the other hand, your child is suffering from low self-esteem and/or depression, the command position may be exactly where the child should be. It provides a sense of control when life appears to have none. You can monitor when the child has reached the point that a move out of this position would be appropriate and wouldn't cause undue stress.

If you have rented a room in your house which happens to be in the command position, or if you have an adult child in this room, you will have a more difficult time establishing your authority. A renter, unless a good friend or a relative, will probably not tolerate a picture of you in their own private space. If the room is furnished with your own furniture, you can maintain a sense of ownership to the area. Even having a picture or print on the wall that belongs to you is a constant reminder to the occupant that this is ultimately your space.

Command position in each room

If occupying the command position(s) in your home is out of the question due to room designations or functionality, then it is wise to be aware of the command position in your own bedroom. As when determining this place in the whole house, you determine the command position of an individual room relative to the entrance door. The back corner furthest away from the entrance to the room is the command position for that particular room. If you cannot occupy this spot in relation to the house in its entirety, you can at least note where it is in your own bedroom. By honoring your authority from the bedroom you can offset what may be sacrificed elsewhere.

In the bedroom, consider what you're keeping in your command position that could be undermining your ownership. This area needs to be free from debris, dirty laundry, waste baskets and hampers. If possible a small chair or rocker could be placed there, keeping the chair empty for your ready use. You don't want your authority sabotaged by a favorite teddy bear. This corner could also simply hold a plant, a favorite painting or something that reminds you of your innate power and beauty.

Finding the command position in your office can also support and enhance your authority. Locate the command position in the dining room and make sure that is where you sit when eating dinner. If the household is led by two parents, both parents need to be in the command spot, side-by-side. Occupy this command chair when conducting family meetings to better establish your voice. Being in the command spot as often as possible is not about manipulating or lording over the other members of your family. It is about you as the adult responsibly assuming the leadership and direction for those people in your charge.

Your bed as a focus

The focus of your bedroom should be your bed. There can, of course, be other furniture in the room, but the bed still needs to be the central piece. In a room where the bed has to compete with armoires, fireplaces, televisions, exotic rugs, computers, and paintings, it can be difficult to maintain your focus on the bed itself.

Canopy beds can be very dramatic and certainly assist in emphasizing the bed as the main piece of furniture. In many instances canopy beds can act as a smaller room in which to sleep. Some people find this very comforting and secure; others find it claustrophobic. If you feel like the whole top will come crashing down upon you during the night, a canopy bed will most likely not work for you.

A bed should also be raised off the floor to allow the flow and circulation you want in life. In addition, nothing should be stored under the bed so that this flow remains unimpeded. If you have to store things under the bed, it is imperative that you put only "soft" items there. These are items that you have an attachment to, that you use and cherish—clothes that you wear, lingerie, love-letters from your current partner, a special quilt from your grandmother. You do not want to store books, guns, old tax documents, scrapbooks from a previous relationship, tools, etc. under your place of repose.

If you choose not to raise your mattress off the floor, you can put a red cloth under it to symbolize the circulation and flow. A futon or other mattress that is intended to be on the floor does not need such an adjustment unless you feel as though you'd like to make one.

Bathroom doors

Many homes are being constructed lately with a master bathroom directly off the master bedroom but with no door in-between. From a Feng Shui standpoint, this is a problem. Bathrooms, particularly a toilet, can drain away money, health and good fortune. It can also drain away energy during your sleep-time when you're most vulnerable. With no door to protect you from this drain, you can predictably wake up from a full night's sleep feeling as tired as when you went to bed.

When there is no door, it is recommended that a "door" of some sort be placed there. If a real, physical door is out of the question, then creativity becomes the solution. Something needs to break the direct line into the bathroom while you're sleeping in your bed. Some type of fabric can be used—a beautiful shear curtain treatment or hand-painted silk panels draped and tied to the sides during the day, or a screen that can be placed in front of the door. There are some exquisitely beautiful beaded curtains that when hanging straight and undisturbed become a colorful scene or pattern, usually of an Asian design. A round faceted crystal can be hung from the ceiling on either side of the doorway to energetically put a door in place. If none of these ideas suit your taste, at least the lid to the toilet needs to be kept down at night.

Even if you cannot see the toilet from your perspective in bed, you are affected by its drain during the night. The secondary drains are also considered in this situation when no door exists between the two rooms. The drains from the sink and from the shower and/or bathtub are not to be totally ignored. If energy drain is a serious and critical problem for you, consider plugging or covering all the secondary drains as well before going to bed.

Placement problems for the toilet

Sleeping with your head against a wall which shares a toilet on the other side drains your energy and sabotages your health on all levels. Since bedrooms are often adjacent to a bathroom, you need to be mindful on which wall the head of your bed goes so that it doesn't back up to a toilet. Likewise, if you sit at your desk with your back to a wall shared with a toilet, you may find yourself getting "pissed off" a lot around work issues. Finally, if cooking food at the stove becomes mixed in with the sounds of a flushing toilet on the other side of the wall, the resulting meal can be less than tasteful.

In any of these cases, if you cannot move the bed, the desk, or the stove, then some other adjustments should be considered. The most logical, aside from moving the furniture, is to place a mirror somewhere on the wall between the toilet and the piece of furniture. If the stove is back-to-back to the toilet, you can place a mirror as a backsplash behind the stove to separate the two elements. Likewise in the bedroom, a mirror could be placed above the headboard of the bed to prevent the toilet from affecting your sleep and health. In the office, if you can't or choose not to move your desk, a mirror on the wall behind you will keep the toilet from polluting your daily affairs.

A smaller mirror could also be used in less obvious ways if you don't want to incorporate a large one. A small round mirror could be fixed to the back of the headboard on your bed or to the back of your chair in your office or behind a picture. It could be placed in a cupboard by the stove if there is no room for a mirrored panel behind the burners. In each situation, the reflective side of the mirror should face *into* the bedroom, the office or the kitchen to complete the separation.

Controlling your office

Just like in the Old West, the Chinese believed that if you ever sat with your back to the front door, you could be in trouble. If you didn't get shot in the back, you'd at the least be startled by someone coming up from behind you. Likewise, the desk being a key piece of furniture in Feng Shui, you don't want to be sitting at your desk in such a way that your back is exposed to anyone coming in through the door.

Most office systems set up an employee in a cubicle which necessitates having a back to the door. Having an underlying sense that someone may frighten you causes your productivity to plummet. There's always an uneasiness that if someone isn't "sneaking up" on you, there will be someone soon. You always feel a need to check over your shoulder. Each time you have to do this, valuable time is lost.

Having a desk facing the entrance door to the office gives a person the sense of being in control. No longer can anyone come up from behind and cause you to jump. No one will be able to "stab you in the back" or "talk behind your back" which are often the metaphors used when feeling vulnerable. Turning the desk around so that you're safely supported by a wall behind you, while your vision is broadened, allows you to be in control in your own space. Being in control brings with it feelings of confidence, safety and strength. Even in a small home office it is often possible to turn the desk around causing the flow of energy to shift. Of course, it may necessitate removal of some file cabinets that aren't used, some storage boxes that never quite made it to the basement, or stacks of books that don't have a home. But being in control means being in control of your space as well as your things.

Too many windows

Large windows can make you feel exposed and overcharged. They allow too much active energy to come in making it difficult to relax and rest. In lake homes this is a feature that is commonly built into the whole side of the house that faces that lake. From anywhere in the cabin/home you can catch a view of the scenery and the lake. And often these large windows are installed in a bedroom if it, too, faces the lake. What happens, in reverse, is that from anywhere on the lake someone can catch a view of you as well. You can be watched while you're reading, watching television, eating, and napping in a chair. Your life is displayed in a fish bowl where you can see the view. In reality, you don't see any more of the lake with these huge windows than if normal-sized windows are used.

When the view is such a predominant part of the lake home, the home itself becomes secondary. It is important to establish some kind of focus inside so that the exterior view works *with* the interior theme, not obliterates it. Having too much of a good thing soon brings about a feeling of complacency regarding its impact. You begin to not appreciate what it can do for you because it's so pervasive. Having windows sized and positioned in proportion with the structure, can provide you with a balance for the space and adequate viewing options. Like having access to too much chocolate, after a while it's taken for granted. You may even begin to question whether or not you like it. If the windows are oversized in a space, they need to be draped or curtained so you have the option of controlling how much impact from the outside you get into your personal space. If curtains are not possible or desirable, make sure you create a safe and secluded spot somewhere else in the house to provide a balance of privacy.

Support

Headboards

A headboard represents a "brace" of sorts that helps you along your journey. This brace or support can come from a spouse, from family, friends, as well as the community. If your headboard is unsteady or occasionally comes completely disengaged from the bedframe, it is a metaphor about your feelings of not having the security you want in life. You never quite relax for fear your support will fail you. It is helpful to make sure that the place where you regenerate yourself and nurture your body (your bed) is safe and worry-free. If the headboard is problematic, it might be time for a new bed.

When your headboard consists of a shelf for the alarm clock, books, knick-knacks, a lamp, etc., you again don't have a good, stable back-up. In fact, your back-up isn't there for your purposes at all but for an entirely different use. Once things start getting set on the shelves, not only does your support leave you but, when you sleep, you have all kinds of energetic activity going on within inches of your head. Electric appliances, such as the alarm clock, emit electromagnetic radiation which is physically harmful. If the headboard cannot be changed, you need to keep it free from unnecessary items. Everything is energy, so be mindful of what sort of energy can be affecting you during your dream time. If the headboard becomes cluttered, so will your dreams. If the headboard needs to be dusted, you may not be thinking clearly about something.

Likewise a footboard helps to stabilize your situation. Many beds do not have a footboard but it is wise to think about having something at the end of the bed to represent one—a chest, a small bench, a wicker basket. You do not want a footboard that rises way up above the bed since that can limit your view on life, but instead one that is just tall enough to give you the added support and foothold you need.

Creating a headboard

If you're sleeping without a headboard, you may be feeling you have no one you can count on. A headboard on your bed gives you a sense of strength and purpose whether that comes from others or from within yourself. If you do not have a headboard you may often feel very alone. A wall is *not* a headboard, nor is a window, nor are a pile of pillows. A headboard is constructed to be a part of the bed; it's solidly fixed to the bed and, when you move the bed, the headboard goes with it. It doesn't matter how high your headboard is as long as you have a place against which you can prop yourself, separate from the wall.

A perfect headboard would be one that is solid with no open slats. Open slats or posts can represent division. If you're sleeping with a partner, a slatted headboard can set up some separation between the two of you. It does not give you the "back-up" you need—there's only intermittent support, not a continual source of strength. If your headboard is slatted or has a series of posts with some open area between them, you need to unify them in some way. Weaving a ribbon or a series of ribbons through all the slats or posts would qualify. Tying some silk cording or ribbon around the middle two slats/posts represent a consolidation between two people.

If you have no headboard, your creative imagination can begin to make one. Hanging a special tapestry or quilt where the headboard would ordinarily be can effectively duplicate one. Draping some beautiful fabric on the wall behind the bed would work. Cutting and painting a piece of cardboard or wood to simulate a headboard would also qualify.

Support

Supporting your child

When a child's room is in front of the front door, they may be experiencing some feelings of isolation. This situation occurs when a front door is inset and not on the same plane as the front wall of the house. Putting a small child in this room can be setting up some fears in them about sleeping alone and having nightmares. They may not even want to go in the room to play or to nap during the day. A room in front of the front door can make a child feel all alone and separated from the rest of the family.

This is a situation that, if at all possible, requires the child be moved to another room in the house. If moving the child is not realistic, you can place a mirror on the wall closest to the rest of the house, reflecting the wall that's furthest away from the house. In effect, you are drawing their bedroom into the main portion of the house and making it part of the whole.

Additionally, it would be good to assure that your child has a solid headboard for the added sense of support in life. Make certain the bed faces the door but is not in the doorway. And check that any chairs in the room are not positioned with their backs to the door.

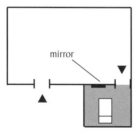

bedroom in front of house

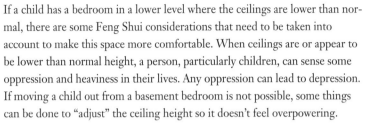

Bedroom problems

If a child has a bedroom in a lower level where the ceilings are lower than normal, there are some Feng Shui considerations that need to be taken into account to make this space more comfortable. When ceilings are or appear to be lower than normal height, a person, particularly children, can sense some oppression and heaviness in their lives. Any oppression can lead to depression. If moving a child out from a basement bedroom is not possible, some things can be done to "adjust" the ceiling height so it doesn't feel overpowering.

Usually in a basement bedroom, natural lighting is minimal due to its lower position. It follows that one of the obvious adjustments is to use as much lighting as possible, particularly torchiere lights which stand on the floor and shoot their light straight up. This movement from the lamp to the ceiling causes the ceiling to look as though it were being pushed higher. One of these lamps in all four corners could be effective, giving it the appearance of pillars holding up the heaviness. Using floor canisters in each of the corners that wash up the walls gives the illusion of elongating the walls so that they appear taller than they really are. Stringing white holiday lights around the upper peripheral of the room also gives a delicate boost to the ceiling.

Mirrors across from any windows can double the amount of daylight that may come in. Keeping the room color a light pastel without going stark white can help to keep the space from being too heavy. Any beams in the bedroom should be painted the same color as the ceiling to minimize the division they cause. Likewise heavy pieces of furniture, such as oversized armoires, big roll-top desks, overstuffed chairs, etc. should be placed somewhere other than the bedroom as they succeed in pulling down and anchoring the feel of the room even more.

Doing Feng Shui for young children

Doing Feng Shui for your small child in their bedroom may be appropriate if there are issues that you want to confront on their behalf. If they are old enough to understand what you're doing, including them will enhance the adjustment. Perhaps they can pick out the kind of mirror you're suggesting, or the color for their walls, or the kind of desk they may want. Once they reach their teen years, it is not fitting to do Feng Shui in their rooms without their permission and participation. If they give you permission, but don't want to participate in the process, the adjustments will not be as effective. If your intention is for their overall protection and well being, you can make some adjustments in the Children area of your own bedroom.

As with any beds, you do not want your child's bed in the doorway, but, instead, away from the direct impact of the door. Yet, when they are lying in bed, they need to be able to see the entry door. Children who are frightened at night will find this position the most secure. They will not have to look around to see if anyone has come into their room or to be afraid that someone will frighten them by coming up from behind. You do not want to position a mirror at the foot of the bed so that if your child were to sit up in the night they see a shadow. This can be a repeated source of fear if they don't recognize what the reflection is, thinking that perhaps someone else is in the room. Additionally, you want your child's bed to have a headboard for an added sense of security and support. These are all features that, as a parent, you can control on behalf of your young child to assist in their health and well-being.

Children's bedrooms

Some health issues and feelings of inferiority can occur in a child if bedrooms are over a garage. A garage is not habitable space, and furthermore it holds pollutants such as lawn mower fuel, paint cans, mineral spirits, and your car. The energy from this space can slowly rise and permeate the rooms above. There's an inordinant amount of activity that comes from the oversized garage door opening and closing several times a day. These features make sleeping over the garage very problematic. It is highly recommended that a child's bedroom be moved if they're currently over a garage. If this is an impossibility, some other measures need to be considered.

When a person, child or not, is suspended over open space, the only way they'll feel better is when there is a safety net under them in case they should fall. A mirror placed under the bed with the reflective side down can help to anchor this child to the earth and provide, if you will, a safety net. Alternatively, the mirror could be placed on the ceiling of the garage under the area in which the bed is located, facing down into the garage. In either case, the mirror, even small in size, reflects and fills in the space so it's not empty and can provide a base for the child.

Another option is to have the child, if old enough, help you locate four rocks or stones. If the child is too small, you may need to do this for them. Place one stone in each corner of the bedroom to anchor the space into the ground. You are, in effect, stabilizing the space so they won't feel as though they're hanging out over an abyss.

Windows in the bedroom

It is difficult to sleep in a room where there's extensive exposure to the outside. Often lake homes will position the master bedroom so that, as you wake up in the morning or fall asleep at night, you can see the view. Having such a dramatic flow of energy from the outside hinders getting a good night's sleep. Unless there are curtains that can be opened and closed, there is little chance of sleeping restfully.

People like to feel safe and cozy in their space, particularly in the bedroom. The bedroom should feel like a nest with enough protection on all sides to give you the safety you need to sleep well. There is always some innate feeling that, if the windows are the floor-to-ceiling type, and without curtains, you could actually fall out. In trying to avoid crashing through the windows in the middle of the night, you may experience something equally as unfortunate, bumping into the furniture.

Additionally, people do not want to sleep so that their heads are "out the window." Using a window as a replacement for a headboard sets up restless nights as well as health issues. Night after night energy is wafting away. If there is no other option than to put the bed below a window, this is one time when blocking off the window is appropriate so that it no longer operates or even looks like a window. In essence, you create a headboard with fabric or wood paneling or some other creative solution with the intention of providing the support and protection of a headboard instead of the openness of a window.

Clocks will keep you on schedule

In order for your life to keep "ticking" along, all the clocks need to work that are displayed in your house. If a malfunctioning clock is sitting in a prominent place in your home, you will constantly be getting the message that some part of your life is also not working. If the clock is in the Partnership area of your home, this is clearly an indication of a partnership not running smoothly. If it's in the Wealth area, something is not moving as it should on the financial front. If your intention is to keep the clock, then it must be repaired.

It's not enough for the clock to be working, it also needs to keep accurate time. Like an old movie where the voice dubbing is about a second behind the actual film, your defective clock can represent a lag somewhere. If you can't rely on your clock to give you an accurate report of the time, your chances of finding support in other areas of your life are minimal. It is important that you wind the clock to keep it as a reliable source of information for you. Whether it's with a key or by pulling the chains on a grandfather clock, your effort in keeping the clock running accurately will keep you on schedule with the rest of your goals and dreams.

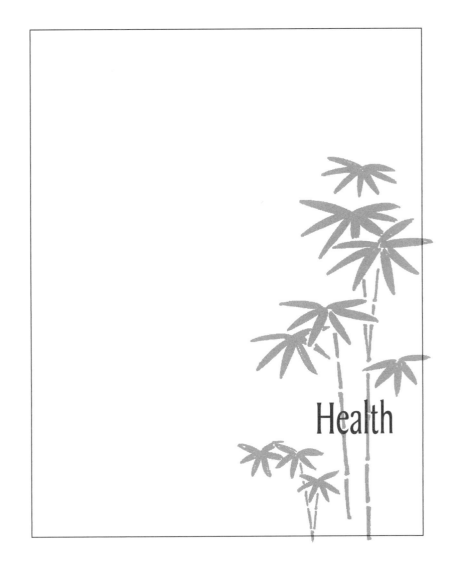

Health

The color yellow

In the Feng Shui tradition the color for health is represented by yellow. Colors are one of many options for adjusting energy in Feng Shui. And sometimes just a touch of the color is all that is needed. If yellow is a favorite color for everyone living or working in the space, consider painting the whole area or one wall in a shade of yellow. If the center point is in a support wall, a print or painting can be hung on one side of the wall with some yellow in it. If a chair is in the center of the space, a yellow pillow may bring the needed representation of health, or perhaps some yellow in a rug under the chair. Tying or fixing a yellow ribbon under the chair works because all things hold an energy whether they're seen or not.

A drop of yellow coloring can also be mixed into a bucket of paint, diluting itself so much that even if the bucket of paint is white, the small amount of yellow will never be detected. Again all things hold an energy whether they're seen or not. Lighting a yellow candle in the Health area is effective. A favorite photo placed in a yellow picture frame can bring in the color. Hanging a crystal with yellow ribbon is another way to enhance good health. Placing a healthy plant in a yellow pot also works.

Another way to bring yellow into your life with a health intention is to wear it. If you don't look good in yellow, wear it underneath. The yellow can also be a yellow lapel pin, a citrine stone necklace, a belt, or a scarf with some yellow in it. Wearing the color with the intention of bringing a "centeredness" to your day can bring phenomenal results to assist you in mirroring a sense of well-being and balance.

Finding the center

The exact center point of your house represents the center point of your life and can determine your state of health. Your state of health is not only your physical well-being but also your emotional, mental and spiritual health. This area can symbolize any feelings of being overwhelmed, stressed, fatigued, depressed, and being out of control. Whenever you're feeling scattered you need to "go back to center," to "get centered." Not only can you do this on an inner level but also in your space.

Knowing where the exact center point is in your home or office enables you to determine what happens there. Once you control the mirror for your health and well being, you begin to get control of your life. When finding the center of your home, all enclosed spaces (spaces with a roof and sides) must be included for measuring—i.e. an attached garage would be included as well as a screened-in porch. On the other hand, a deck would not be included nor a porch that may have a roof but no sides. Finding the center of your space is analogous to finding its heartbeat.

Aligning with the center assists in all the other areas of your life. As you may well know, if you're not feeling well or if you're stressed, these feelings affect all other aspects of your life—your job may suffer, your partnership may suffer, relationships with friends and family may be in jeopardy. Not feeling well inhibits your ability to make money and to maintain a clear vision for your life. It is important to locate this Health area so you can get a handle on what's happening at your center. Whether it's in a closet, in a bathroom, in the middle of your living room or inside a support wall, the important thing is that you have located it. Just your knowing where the center is changes your consciousness about the space in which you're operating.

Honoring the center

If you calm your center, you calm your life. This is true with regard to a meditation practice. If you incorporate some type of meditation or meditative activity such as yoga, walking, or breathing exercises, you will find that this serenity and peace will exude into the rest of your life. You handle life's challenges with less panic and pandemonium. Likewise, finding the center of your space, calming it or honoring it in some way, will start to bring serenity within the walls.

If you locate the center of your house and realize that it's in a closet, that closet holds an importance that you've probably overlooked. In this case, "calming the center" may take the form of cleaning the closet of useless items, purging out old things to enable a flow of healthy energy to settle in. If the center falls in a bathroom, keeping the lid down on the toilet is the least that could be done. In addition, putting a small round mirror on the ceiling above the toilet with the reflective side facing down toward the toilet keeps the health from being flushed away. A plant can be set on the back of the toilet tank (a lovely silk one is fine) to symbolize vitality and life in this area.

If the Health area is in a hallway or in the middle of a room, hanging a small round faceted crystal is the suggested way to mark the center. The crystal can be hung close to the ceiling with clear fish line which would not generally be noticeable to visitors or guests. If the Health area is in a supporting wall you have the option of deciding which side of the wall you want to use to represent the center point. On either side you can place a small table on which items representing happiness and viability are arranged. Adjusting the energy in a positive way in your Health area brings about a serene, well-adjusted environment.

Healthy enhancements

In setting up the center of your space to reflect your health and well-being, select only those items that will mirror to you feelings of delight, beauty and balance. A crystal hung from the ceiling can take unbalanced, distorted energy and reflect it back out as beautiful rainbows spread across the room. A fountain set in the middle of a space can dramatically represent life and energy with both the sound and the water motion. Even if the center point of the space is in a cupboard, meaningful things can happen around the issue of health. Aside from keeping the cupboard maintained (cleaned and sorted), a special item can be placed inside to represent the point of balance. A small vase with silk flowers might be set there so that whenever you open the cupboard door you are reminded of your intention.

A photo of a special moment is always effective as a health adjustment—your wedding picture, a picture of your children as babies, a wonderful vacation, a picture of a special friend. Whatever the photo, make sure it conjures up happy, joyful memories. If you become sad, wistful, or melancholy when you look at the picture, it is not a good trigger for harmony and balance. Also overdoing the number of photos can set up additional busyness and scattered energy. One special photo usually works best, with the option of exchanging it for another one every so often.

Lighting a candle in the Health area signifies a steadiness as well as a sense of warmth and security. When lighting a candle make sure you do not leave it unattended. It is not "good" Feng Shui if your house burns down. Harnessing the element of fire in a controlled setting such as a candle represents the harness we're trying to create in our lives so things don't get out of control. When you light a candle you're sending a core message about taking charge of your life.

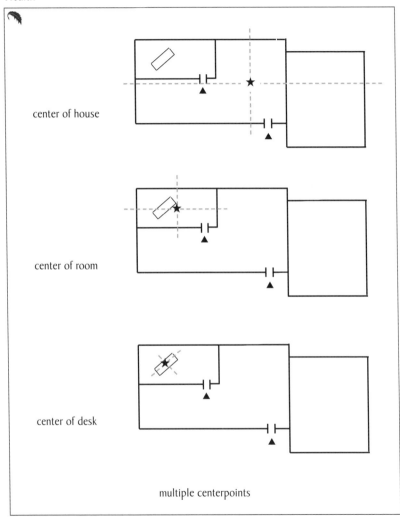

center of house

center of room

center of desk

multiple centerpoints

Multiple centerpoints

If health becomes an issue in your life, working in as many centerpoints as possible will up your chances of making changes in this area. For example, adjusting the energy in the center point of your whole house is an obvious action. It is also appropriate to adjust the energy in the center point of just your bedroom. Some bedrooms have a light or a fan in the middle of the room from which a small round faceted crystal can be hung. But in recent years many bedrooms are being built without this feature, instead opting for recessed lights or lighting from other sources altogether. So other alternatives need to be explored.

If the bed extends into the center of the room, which may happen in a smaller bedroom, something can be placed on the bed under the center point to signify to you a perfect state of health—a special quilt (maybe with some yellow in it to intensify the intention), a shawl, a pillow. If placing an object on top of the bed is too bothersome, then a special item can be placed under the bed to adjust and enhance the health energy—a special little gift box that may contain some of your treasured mementos, a quilt (that may be used as needed but always replaced under the bed in the center point of the room), a book that holds special significance to you with regard to this particular health issue, even silk flowers can be placed under there. If you have built-in storage drawers under the bed, be mindful of placing something in the appropriate drawer with the intention of holding your health as its reflection—a special extravagant sachet, lingerie, a shawl.

By using as many center points in the space as you can around your health issue, it will not only remind you repeatedly of your focussed intention, but will also assist you in tapping into the main source of this energy on many levels, bringing about the healing you deserve.

Bathrooms in the center

True to its purpose, a bathroom drains things away, but it can also drain away your energy, your health, and your money. Indoor bathrooms, although a necessary part of our lives, can be a challenge depending upon their location in your space. Anytime a bathroom (particularly the toilet) is visible from some other area of the house or office, there is potential for something being "flushed away" in your life.

When a toilet is in the middle of your house, this sets up the probability of some health issues in the family. These health issues can take the form of physical ailments as well as mental, emotional and spiritual difficulties. Additionally when a toilet is in the center or the "hub" of your house, it can affect all aspects of your life, not just your health. It stands to reason that when you're not feeling well, everything else in your life will not flow as smoothly—your job is jeopardized, your partnerships are strained, relations with friends and family are stressed.

To soften the impact of this toilet placement, keep the lid of the toilet down when not in use and the door to the bathroom closed. In addition, place a mirror on the outside of the bathroom door to prevent your energy from going down the toilet. If health has become a major concern in your family, put a mirror on all four walls of the bathroom to disperse the flushing energy of the toilet and to keep good health, well-being and balance in your space.

Prominent bathrooms

If the first thing you see upon entering your home is a bathroom, your health may be seriously affected, particularly with bladder and kidney issues. Seeing the bathroom when you first enter can typically encourage you to use it. Soon, every time you enter your home you'll have to use the bathroom. Eventually you begin to think about having to use the bathroom before you get home so there becomes a sense of urgency. Finally you have to use the bathroom upon entering anybody's home because that's what your system has become accustomed to. Whether your bathroom is near the front door or the door that you use the most often, which may be a side door or a door coming in from the garage, this condition can occur.

The doors to these bathrooms need to be kept closed so you won't have the constant trigger to use it each time you walk into your house. A mirror on the outside of the bathroom door will also deflect the energy. In designing a home, keep in mind the dilemma of having bathrooms so close to entrances and intentionally place them some distance from the doors so their impact is diminished.

Likewise, having a bathroom right off the living room can encourage this unfortunate condition as well, especially if the actual toilet is in full view of the living room's perspective. Once again the simplest adjustment is to keep the door to the bathroom closed.

Hallways and your intentions

To ease any intestinal problems, close the door to a bathroom that is at the end of a long hallway. A long hallway gets energy moving very fast and forcefully, like a train picking up speed. When this energy ends up in the toilet it affects your digestive system. A mirror could be placed on the outside of the bathroom door to deflect the energy away from the toilet. If in doing this, however, the length of the hallway seems to extend further to you, then place something else on the door—a wreath of silk flowers, a tapestry, paint the door a different color, paint an image on the door such as a tree, a design, or a favorite vacation scene.

In addition, add a "speed deterrent" to the center of the hallway to slow the energy down in the first place so it doesn't hit the bathroom door with such force. This "speed deterrent" may take the form of a round faceted crystal hung from the ceiling in the middle of the hallway. A mobile could also achieve this, or a windchime. Whatever is placed in the hall to soften this energy needs to be something you enjoy seeing or experiencing. If it becomes something you're annoyed with or don't find particularly appealing, then your intention of easing some internal health issues may not be as effective.

Bathrooms near the kitchen

If your toilet is too close to the kitchen, you may be cooking with unhealthy "ingredients." Bathrooms do not belong above the kitchen or directly off the kitchen. There's an important separation that is imperative to good health to keep the bathroom energy from affecting your cooking endeavors in the kitchen.

If a bathroom is right off the kitchen, the door must be kept closed at all times. If a pet is accustomed to going in there to use a litter box or drink water, it is recommended that the litter box or source of water be moved to another area completely or that a pet door be installed so the animal can come and go with the door still being kept closed. Additionally, it is not a bad idea to hang a mirror on the outside of the bathroom door to reinforce its "disappearance" from the kitchen area.

If a bathroom is situated above a kitchen, again there's the possibility of jeopardizing your health by mixing the toilet energy with the kitchen energy. More specifically if the stove is directly beneath the toilet, there's a potential problem. Once again a small mirror can "separate" the two elements. By placing a mirror (reflective side down) on the floor behind the toilet you can successfully create a barrier between these two appliances. If that doesn't seem like it would be workable, the mirror can be attached to the ceiling above the stove or placed in a cupboard above the stove, the reflective side still down, to symbolize the break.

Prominent kitchens

When the kitchen is the first room you see when you enter the front door of your home, there's a tendency to develop eating disorders or digestive problems. Your attention is drawn to food as soon as you walk into your space. This may mean there's a tendency to over eat or to over indulge in snacks. It may also manifest in digestive disorders and into an unhealthy preoccupation with food. It also signifies that people in your life come to eat your food and then leave. There is not the support and loyalty you'd expect from good friends. You may find you "nourish" others without reciprocal treatment.

It is important to minimize the impact of seeing the kitchen when entering. If it's possible, install a door that can be kept closed so that your eye does not take you directly into the kitchen. If a door can't be hung, try draping fabric or hanging a curtain to close up the doorway. If none of those things seem to be workable, then make sure you have something close by that attracts your attention and diverts you from going into the kitchen. A dramatic centerpiece, a fountain, a sculptural piece, a rug—anything that "runs interference" with the kitchen will help to keep the digestive, eating problems to a minimum.

White and light in the kitchen

White is the preferred color for kitchens. Although extensive use of white in other rooms can be problematic, in the kitchen the color white contrasts with the food. It acts as a canvas for the artistic presentation of meals. White maintains a clean, sanitary look and gives the impression of a healthy preparation area. White can be accented with another color to ease its starkness. You may want to pull in a color from the dining room or living room as an accent which will tie the kitchen into the theme of the whole space.

Letting as much natural sunlight into the area as possible activates a good flow of energy. With white as the main color, the sunlight can be reflected and enhanced in the kitchen. If additional lighting is needed, under-the-counter lighting can add an element of drama. If the cupboards do not go all the way to the ceiling providing a ledge, this is another area in which a soft glow of lights could be installed. Rather than crowd the upper ledge with knick-knacks, baskets, plates, plants or storage of miscellaneous things that don't fit anywhere else, one or two decorative items with lighting behind them provide an elegant and dramatic look.

Your desk and your health

Using your desk or any other horizontal surface (dresser, table-top, shelf) to access various life issues can be an effective reminder of your intentions. In a microcosmic version of your house or office, you can use the center of your desk to render some changes in health and well being. Using the center, where you probably do most of your work, presents some interesting yet powerful challenges. The most obvious is how you place an object in the center of your desk without it continually getting in your way while working. The solution is that twice a day you move the item—once in the morning when you sit down at your desk, again in the afternoon when you leave for the day.

If you place an object in the middle of your desk to represent your health issue, it can take the form of a crystal paperweight, a favorite stone, a plant, a bell, a photo, or whatever else speaks to you of health and vibrancy in a balanced, harmonious way. Each morning upon arriving at your desk, you can ceremoniously remove the item and place it out of the way, doing the reverse at the end of the workday. The intention with which you do this activity twice a day will dramatically focus on what you're calling in. Every time you do your "mini ceremony" you're consciously reinforcing your intention. Continually forgetting to replace the object may be a statement about the strength of your goal.

This activity can become part of your routine for a limited period of time—either nine or twenty-seven days (nine being a very powerful number in Feng Shui)—requiring commitment and dedication to a focussed intention. When a serious health issue strikes, or feelings of desperation around life's complications and frenzy occur, doing a small directed activity for a certain period of time elicits a sense of empowerment and control.

Your furnace and your health

If your furnace is in the middle of your house, it may be burning up your health. Furnaces, by nature, are meant to generate heat—you need them and are grateful for them when the temperatures drop below zero. Yet, a furnace can very easily get out of control and burn up anything in its way. In Feng Shui, a furnace in the middle of a space burns up the energy of health—physical health as well as mental, emotional, and spiritual health.

It is necessary to "tend the fire" of the furnace so you have heat but not at the expense of your well-being. You want to bring some element of water near the furnace to prevent "burn out." This water element can take the form of a plant—probably silk since a real one would have a hard time growing in a basement or dark space. The intention of a plant is to be watered (even silk plants hold an intention of being real). The amount of water needed to water a plant is enough to keep the furnace fire in check. A silk plant can be set on the floor near the furnace or silk vines can be wound around it and/or the ductwork.

If the plant idea doesn't feel appropriate, you can put a small mirror on top of the furnace (reflective side down). A mirror represents the water element. Originally mirrors were reflecting pools in which people could see themselves. The mirror can be round, two to three inches in diameter, and placed on top of the furnace or ductwork. In the Chinese Five Element Theory, the color for water is black, so something black can be put on or near the furnace—black cloth or ribbon can be draped on the furnace and/or ductwork.

Alternatively, you can place a fountain on the floor in the room directly above the furnace. Something bearing the color black can also be used (a black chair, a black rug, etc.). Likewise a plant can be strategically positioned above the unit to temper the fires from below.

Your car's message

Just like your home, your car is an extension of yourself. If it's "running on fumes" and in need of fuel, chances are that you are in need of regenerating as well. If the brakes squeal reminding you of the potential of a brake failure when you least expect it, you may be risking a "brake" down. It may be time to slow down and stop running. If there's a slow oil leak under the hood, you, too, may be experiencing some leakage of energy or time in your life. Any oil change or tune-up is indicative of regenerating your own resources to help you run better and smoother.

If the tires are low or bald, it's harder for you to get ahead—you can't get the traction you need. If the windshield has a crack running across it, your vision around some issue may be impaired—you can't see the situation clearly. If the exhaust system is causing some problems, check to see if it might not reflect some digestive problems you're dealing with. If the starter goes out, you may find your energy to initiate some changes may be at an all time low. Get the starter fixed and you can once again rev up your life.

To help your car run better you might try naming it. Anything that you name (your house, your computer, your favorite armchair) runs better and lasts longer because you now relate to it on a personalized basis and form an intimate connection with it. The more you use your car's name, the better its overall energy will be. You will be more inclined to take care of problems as soon as they come up and before they become major if you realize their impact on your own life. Dealing with problems on your automobile with determined assertiveness will reflect to you a method of dealing with your own problems.

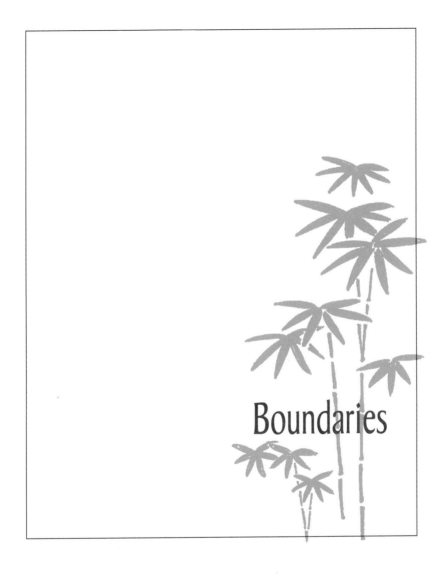

Boundaries

Living by a busy street

Living by a busy city street or a highway can bring the speed and fast movement into your own space. When you can hear cars and trucks zooming past day and night, your life begins to enter into this activity. You begin to resonate to the frenzy taking place right in front of your home over and over again. Even if you can't hear the traffic sounds, the motion is still there and you can feel its presence. Too much activity is like a whitewater rapids—at first it's rather scintillating and can make you feel "on your way." But after a while it becomes tiresome and positively frustrating. Often you don't realize how it has gotten on your nerves until you get away from it. Having property on a beautiful quiet lake away from the city noise can be a great way to rejuvenate from living in an urban setting.

But if a lake home is not an option for you, then a home near a busy road needs protection from the constant movement. A fountain on the inside will provide white noise to minimize the effects of the traffic sounds. See to it that all bedrooms that are used regularly for sleeping are in the back of the house to assure the quietest space possible.

In front of the house, you may want to install a fence to visually block the sight of the traffic or at least some hedges to afford you some privacy. You may also want to situate a large boulder in front of the house or a tree to anchor your space into the earth. With the intense activity going on in the road, it's easy to get caught up in its momentum. Something heavy to anchor you into the ground will help to slow you down to a more manageable pace. From the inside a curtain treatment can be used to mask off the traffic. Even sheers over the windows will keep the visual to a minimum yet still allow light into your space.

Each room has a focus

Most people use spare rooms as junk rooms—they're undefined and have no specific purpose. All kinds of things are stored here with no definite activity in mind. If located in the Partnership area of the house, it's common to see serious commitment issues with regard to a partner. The Feng Shui theory is that each room is set up for one activity: the kitchen is for preparing food (not working out); the dining room is for eating (not doing office work); the bedroom is for sleeping and intimacy (not working on the computer or watching television). It also follows that each room should be a different color with different floor treatment to symbolize this division of activities. Although most homes do not follow this design statement, the furniture and accessories tend to dictate what happens in each room.

A spare room is often where things end up when there's nowhere else to put them—you might see a sewing machine, a treadmill, a futon, maybe a bookcase, or stacks of boxes piled on extra chairs. What do you do in this room? Each room needs a focus activity. Maybe it's primarily a sewing room where all the items required to sew are accessible. The futon adds a softer element where you can do handsewing. It can also be pulled out for the occasional guest. The treadmill is moved somewhere else or draped to minimize its presence except when in use. All extra unused things are neatly stacked in the closet. Maybe the room is primarily used as a workout room. Then, of course, the treadmill is the focus, minimizing the sewing machine. All accessories required for this work out area would be available—a full-sized mirror, boom box, towels, etc.

Giving a room definition symbolizes setting your own boundaries. As you can see it doesn't mean other peripheral or secondary activities can't go on in that room, but the main purpose has been clearly defined for its use.

Problem neighbors

If your neighbor is problematic for whatever reason, you can protect yourself and send their energy back. A problem neighbor could be someone who has a barking dog, or someone who throws late-night parties on a regular basis. It could be someone who keeps the yard piled with old cars, half-finished construction projects, recycling, and unidentified junk. A problem neighbor could also be an over-sized house that seems to bear down on you and your family. It could be a church, a synagogue, a funeral home, or a cemetery (all of which exude sadness, sometimes devastation due to the gravity of someone's death). It could be a tall apartment building. In any of these cases, you want to protect yourself and your space from the negative influences that are coming from next door, across the street, or above.

To soften the impact from the chaos and negativity, place a small mirror in a window or on a wall with the reflective side facing towards the offending neighbor. You, in short, are sending the offensive energy back from where it came, leaving your space clear and protected. The mirror can be a very small round one propped or hung in the window or placed behind a picture. A convex mirror could turn the image upside down weakening its impact on you even further.

In order for this to work it is imperative that you come from a compassionate and sincere place in your heart. Any hatred or anger must be resolved before doing this adjustment, otherwise, all attempts to alleviate a difficult situation can backfire. This adjustment may open up channels for better communication between you and your neighbor to help solve the problem or it may mysteriously cause your neighbor to improve their situation without any communication on your part. In any event, it will protect you from taking on the direct influence of whatever is being directed toward your space.

Reclaiming a home

If one of the partners of a divorce remains in the home that they originally purchased or acquired together, there can always be reminders of the relationship and its problems. It is important that the partner who continues to live in the house reclaim it as his or her own and release its original intention as a shared space. If a woman goes back to her maiden name, all indications of the married name need to be removed, such as on the mailbox, welcome mats, door knockers, etc. Any wedding gifts with the old initials engraved into them such as wine goblets or monogrammed towels should be recycled or given away.

In addition, ideally, the bedroom set should be replaced, particularly if there is any interest in nurturing another relationship. If an entire new bedroom set is financially not possible, the mattress and bed springs should be replaced. If that is not financially feasible, at least new sheets, pillowcases, and pillows need to be purchased.

In a space where a couple has lived together and where now only one remains, decisions have to be made as to what items of furniture can comfortably remain and which ones will be a constant reminder of the pain of the break-up. If you cannot afford to replace furniture, get rid of what you can and put throw covers or slip covers over the rest to mask their original look. Even putting new pillows on an old sofa can give it a "new" look. It is important to make the space yours alone if you've acquired a house due to a divorce. The same principles apply if you've inherited a house from your family. Bring in your favorite color as much as you can and ring the doorbell each time you come through your front door to establish your voice as the owner and keeper of this little part of the universe.

Your home office

If your office is at home, you must exercise mindfulness so that your "office" energy doesn't spill over into your personal life. More and more people are enjoying the convenience of working out of the home. Entire magazines are written about this phenomenon; workshops are presented on the home office. People have come to see the advantages of no commute to work, the wardrobe convenience, and being close to the family if needed. The computer, fax machines, and modems have all made this possible.

From a Feng Shui viewpoint there are some potential concerns. Most importantly is the occurrence of knowing when it's quitting time and whether there are "after-hours" policies. Although working at home at a job you love seems like a dream come true, it's important that it not take over your life.

One main Feng Shui principle is balance. Even though you may love your job, there still needs to be a balance in your life. If you love to garden and all you talk about is gardening, look at seed catalogs and go to flower shows, anyone else may find you quite tiresome. It's the same situation if you get buried in your work. Other interests are needed to help balance you out. When you have an office at home you need to confine its energy. The work needs to be in a room with a door which can be closed when you're done working. Using the dining room table as your desk is invasive to your family and, if there is no family, it's invasive to your own personal existence. Having your office in your bedroom really invades your personal life.

Being able to physically leave your office is an important factor. If your office is part of your living room or at one end of your kitchen, then throw a beautiful silk scarf over the desk or drape the computer so you visually see when your business is "open" and when it is "closed."

Designated private space

When children have to share a bedroom with another child or two, each child needs to designate a personal space. If possible, try to screen off each sleeping area or put some kind of divider between each area. In a small bedroom this is often not possible or practical so then some other means of designating private space should be determined. Each child could have a private space somewhere else in the house to be alone, without interruptions. Even a simple shelf can be "off limits" to other people where a child could put personal things; no one else would interfere or touch any of these private items.

When a child doesn't experience the concept of boundaries, there is a possibility that later in life that child will become territorial, not sharing anything with anybody. The ramifications of this kind of behavior in a marriage or a significant relationship are destructive. All possessions take on such inordinant importance that letting go of any of them is impossible. Likewise, when there are no rules about what belongs to whom, the child may feel entitled to everything, not realizing that this, too, is unacceptable behavior.

The boundary concept supports the Feng Shui idea of sacred space. Everyone needs some sacred place to call their own where no one else will trespass unless asked. What is kept in this sacred space is likewise sacred. When a child doesn't experience what sacredness is and doesn't understand when something is special, then nothing is sacred or special.

Defining your space

When separating projects or ongoing activities that take place in the same vicinity, the placement of rugs can do an effective job. A rug can create an entry when there is none so that visitors feel like there is some transition place in which to set things down, take off coats, remove boots, etc. before going into the living room. A rug under a desk differentiates the office area from the sleeping area in a space that is used as both an office and a guest room. Rugs situated in a studio apartment can help visitors as well as the occupant know where they are and what happens where.

Plants also help to define a space. A couple of large plants standing about three to four feet apart can create a doorway. With the help of a screen you can beautifully build an office space for yourself—or a bedroom area. A row of plants can direct the flow of traffic and can set boundaries. If tall and lush enough they can even provide a certain amount of privacy.

Fabric also delineates specific events. Simply hung on a curtain rod, beautifully flowing panels create a door, walls, or both. Hung from the ceiling, hand-painted fabric dramatically enhances a setting with draping and knots, ties and tassels. In defining your space with whatever method, you create a system of living that clarifies what you do and gives you a map for inviting in change.

A freestanding screen can be functional as well as beautiful, helping to diminish the impact of various endeavors. A screen set in front of a desk and computer will calm a space enough so that it can effectively be a bedroom. Set in front of a spare bed, it diminishes the feelings of working in a bedroom and of wanting to nap on a regular basis.

Acquiring antiques

Furnishings are an important factor in looking at the Feng Shui of a space. How they're placed, what they look like, and what purpose they serve are all elements in creating a productive, harmonious space. Many people are enamored with antiques purchased from antique stores, estate sales, garage sales, or inherited from the family. Having antiques can attractively enhance a space especially if there are some fond memories attached to them.

However, antiques can be just as problematic as beneficial. In some cases, the furniture has been moved cross-country, crammed in with an already furnished home, and left there because of guilt or feelings of responsibility. If you get rid of this "special gift," it is your perception that other members of the family would be upset and/or hurt. "What would Mother say if I got rid of Grandma's pedestal sewing machine?" "This upright piano doesn't hold a tune anymore, but it has been in the family for years." "When Aunt Thelma comes to visit, she'd be hurt if she didn't see us using the lava lamp she gave us." In all likelihood these inherited pieces eventually become a burden as resentments build around having to keep things that are not wanted.

On the other hand, it is very advantageous to have heirlooms that remind you of a friend or relative who was near and dear to your heart. If they were successful in their lives—and not just financially successful but successful in living their lives with joy and purpose—then having a daily reminder of their spirit is very auspicious. Refinishing or re-upholstering the piece facilitates your claim of some of the memories and enhances the pleasant associations you have with the person, whether living or not. Using a beautiful antique in your home or office, particularly if you knew the previous owner, helps to tie to you an ancestral lineage that speaks to your roots and where you've come from.

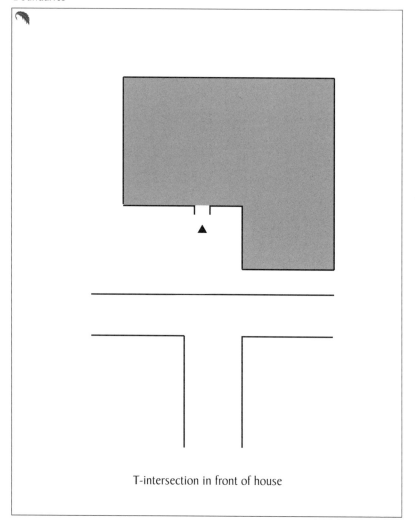

T-intersection in front of house

House at a "T" intersection

A house at the end of a "T" intersection is constantly bombarded by energy coming down the road and ending up at the front door. This condition leaves the homeowners tired, drained and overwhelmed. There is always an innate fear that the cars coming down the road toward your home may have brake failure and end up in your living room. If a bedroom is in the front of the house, the person who sleeps in that room may never sleep restfully or peacefully while living in that house. The house at the end of a "T" intersection is being hit by too much, too quickly. Life here may be too frantic for most people.

If the view from your front door is a road aiming straight toward you, it is highly recommended that you position a protective barrier between your home and the road. This barrier can be a row of trees or hedges. It can be a large boulder or a series of smaller ones on the front lawn. Consider installing a fence running the full width of your lot in front. A fountain is also an effective tool. On a more subtle level you can position two animal guardians on either side of your front door—two lions, gargoyles or any animals of your choice. Obviously these two statues won't stop a car going 60 miles per hour from crashing through your front door, but neither will a hedge or a fence. The point is that you have set your energetic boundary to enable you to live in this house without the constant nagging thought that you're going to have unexpected visitors.

Clarity

Focal points

Each room should have one main focus to which your eye is drawn. When your eye doesn't know what to look at first, there's confusion. You assist this by providing a central element in the room—maybe two if it's a large enough space. This focal point can be a floral arrangement in the living room or a special painting over the fireplace. It can be a rug or a sofa which adds some drama. In a bedroom it is the bed. In the dining room it is the dining room table.

Once your eye has an anchor it can move about more easily and take in whatever else is happening in the space. In order to create drama, there will be some items that aren't as memorable as others. The contrast between the intensity of a special piece and the less intensity of others is what makes this piece stand out. If everything were dramatic, there would be no drama. Even the simpler pieces, however, need to be good quality, in good repair, and should all match. As in music, every note is important but there's usually a build-up to a climactic part which gives the musical piece movement and direction. In your space you also want to create this movement and Feng Shui flow by having a climactic point.

Displaying photos

When there's too much to look at in a space, your eyes get tired, your senses scatter and, as a result, you feel overwhelmed. One particular situation that people seem to enjoy but don't realize how draining it can be is the "photo wall." The photo wall usually starts out to be the simple story of the family who lives there, but ends up spreading into an epic covering every square inch from floor to ceiling. If you're seeing this photo wall for the first time you don't know what to look at first. It's almost like being in an art gallery where you'd expect this kind of momentum. In your home, where you spend time every day, it's too tiring to be bombarded by this impact.

Each photo holds an energy and a story on its own. When there are multitudes of photos all vying for attention, it can get rather "noisy" on an energy level. No one can appreciate any of the photos for what they are. Imagine what it would be like if just one or two pictures were hung where you could actually stop for a moment to soak in their meaning. Imagine what it would be like to absorb the expression from the photo and to "get into" the spirit with which it was taken. Imagine what it would be like to relive the moment again and again through the photo. This can't happen very well when there are other distractions and other "voices" calling out.

Having photos of friends and family exhibited can work very well in a home. The principles of Feng Shui propose simplicity and serenity. In order to accommodate your need to have a photo wall, consider putting up your favorite two or three for a week or a month. After that, replace with other photos that are your next favorites and continue until you cycle back to the beginning again. Not only does it eventually exhibit all your special pictures, but it also makes you very mindful and aware of what you have on your walls, so that each and every photo becomes important.

Split-level entries

If the first thing you have to do upon entering your home is to decide whether to go up or down, you have a split-level home. The word "split" gives you an indication of potential problems with this kind of entrance. Not only are you divided in your own mind about which direction to take when you come through the front door, but it affects the general cohesiveness of people who live there or come to visit. There's a tendency for argumentation between family members, resulting in issues between partners as well as children. Having a split level feature also results in inability to make clear, concise decisions. Every decision is a labored, agonizing process. Having guests come to your home and not know where to go is another pattern of indecision.

To alleviate the influences of this kind of entry, the element of indecision can be addressed by directing your eye toward a focus, positioning the focal point in the area where you'd want people to go. For instance, if your living room is on the upper level of a split level home, putting something at the top of the stairs to draw your eye will begin the flow in that direction. A colorful painting or print with a spotlight emphasizing its position will draw someone up the stairs. A beautiful plant, a sculptural piece, or a small table with a lamp on it can elicit the attention needed so people will be drawn in the correct direction.

To soften the effects of argumentation, you might hang some silk green vines on the post that divides the two stairways. A ribbon or silk cording, even some beautiful fabric, may also accomplish the task. Your goal is to mask the influence of the divisive post that cuts things in two. Hanging a crystal in the entry can also eliminate the negativity of a split entrance. The crystal can be hung from an existing light fixture or directly from the ceiling with the intention of eliminating all indecision and argumentative inclinations.

Split entries

If you stand inside your front door with one eye looking down a long hallway and the other eye being stopped by a wall, you have a split entry. Similar to a split level, there's indecision as to where to look. When your eyes are bouncing between two distance points, this becomes very tiring and distracting. When you're in disarray at home it affects your performance at work. When you are less creative and productive at work, it could affect your income. So you can see, a split entry affects many aspects of your life and is best avoided if at all possible.

When you have such a situation, determine a focus to which your eyes will always be drawn. Having something attractive or beautiful by the wall closer to the entry will eliminate the need to move your eyes all over looking for somewhere to land. A tall lush plant can act as a focus. Painting the wall a different color, or wallpapering with a striking, dramatic pattern, can also bring your eyes to a consensus. A vase placed on a pedestal might be attractive to you.

Likewise, if you want the focus to be down the hall, similar arrangements can be used—a large plant, a sculptural piece, your favorite painting with a light on it, a small table with a decorative mirror hanging above it. In this case, you want to have both eyes focus on the object in the distance. Your imagination and creativity can determine not only what to use but also in which of the two areas to place it.

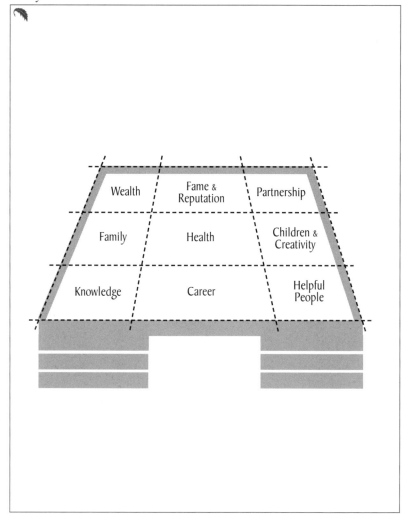

Your desk and your life

The top of your desk is a map of your life. Where you stack things, how you care for your desk, what you keep there can all tell a story about your priorities, your patterns, and your passions. The truth is that any horizontal surface can become a map for your life—a cluttered dresser top, a credenza whose top you can no longer see, a nightstand piled with books. What applies to the desk will apply to any other "tops" of things you may operate from.

If you cannot see the top of your desk, you cannot clearly see the vision for your life. If, as you sit at your desk, a plant has died that was sitting in the upper left corner, money is probably not "growing" for you. If items that need to be filed are stacked here and there, you can experience that feeling of being at "loose ends." If your computer takes up most of the space on your desk, you have not left yourself any room to be creative.

Your desk needs to be clear and clean. Deal with the loose ends. Toss out the dead things—whether they're plants or projects that didn't happen. File what needs to be filed. If you cannot access easily what's on your desk, there are aspects of your life that you cannot access easily as well. If you stack "things to do later" in the upper right corner of your desk, which is the Partnership area—think about the message you're giving yourself around getting a partner, maintaining a partner, or resolving any partnership issues, whether personal or business. Check your desk both at home and at work to see what message it's giving you and begin to change any messages you don't want to be receiving.

Lighting to enhance your space

If you want to use lighting to enhance your space, the most important thing to remember is that all burnt out light bulbs need to be replaced as soon as possible. If you have a lamp or light that doesn't work, it's like having a clock that doesn't keep time. Neither one is good to have around while in an unworkable state.

Any kind of lighting can be used to create change in your life. If you wanted to bring about some new growth possibilities in your career, you can place a large plant with a floor canister behind it in the Career area of your house. Or you can string holiday lights throughout a large plant in the Career area to lighten and spark the job shift.

If you want to bring in a partner, placing two candles in the Partnership area of your bedroom represents a flame being sparked between two people. When lighting the two candles, light one from a match or another source of fire and then light the second candle from the first to represent the connection. If money is your challenge, use a lamp, track lighting, or a spotlight to emphasize some element of water in the Wealth area of your home—a fountain with a light shining on it, a painting depicting water with a directional lamp highlighting it, or an aquarium which has its own lighting from within. If you want to lift a low basement ceiling, use a torchiere lamp to shine the light upward, pushing the ceiling higher. You could also string some holiday lights horizontally around the periphery of the room where the ceiling and the wall meet to lift the energy.

Lighting, used wisely and creatively, can enhance your space and your life. If you're deliberate about where the sources of light are placed, you begin to "see" more clearly around an issue and can be "en-light-ened" around a goal or vision.

Special effects with light

A space's energy is altered when artificial lighting is introduced or changed. Whether it's a lamp, a sconce, candles, a floor canister, track lighting, holiday lights, or a torchiere floor lamp, lighting brings life to a dark, stagnant corner. It accentuates a hallway, emphasizes a plant or a sculptural piece of art; lighting lifts a ceiling that's becoming oppressive or a beam that divides. It helps to differentiate your house from everyone elses. Lighting softens a space or enlivens a dark room, depending on the final result you want to achieve.

Lighting serves a function by enabling you to see when it's dark outside. But more than that, it creates your space and sets the tone or mood. Lighting needs to be appropriate to the task—if you want to read, obviously the lights need to be bright enough. Likewise, if you want to relax, talk, or have a romantic evening with someone, bright lights would be inappropriate. Dimmer switches and three-way bulbs enable you to create different moods in the same setting.

Sometimes you may want peripheral lighting that adds to the ambiance but doesn't enable you to read or do needlework. Candles serve this purpose as can holiday lights. Whatever the source or intensity of the light, it moves the energy in that part of the room. Be mindful of what area of your space (and of your life) you are illuminating each and every time you turn on the lamp or plug in the lights. Practicing Feng Shui, you can "shed some light" on an aggravating and perplexing dilemma.

Candles with intention

Whenever you use a candle, you are en-"lightening" a space, a corner, an altar, or yourself. The intentional lighting of a candle brings illumination—that may be physical light or shedding light on a particular issue. Using candles can help bring you back to your center because their flame is soft, quiet, and warm. A candle adds atmosphere—a candle-lit dinner is romantic; a wedding by candlelight is elegant; a candlelight procession is dramatic. Using a candle for your intention adds all of these elements and more.

If you want to use a candle for your intention, you can also burn one in the color relating to your issue. For example, around money issues, use a purple or lavender candle. Light two pink candles on the dining room table for relationship. Burn a white candle to keep your creativity sparked. For deep contemplative work, use a blue candle. For your health and general well being, a yellow or an off-white candle is appropriate. If you want to get some things moving in your life, a grouping of red candles will do that for you.

Like aquariums and fountains, candles do require a certain amount of maintenance. Candleholders need to be filled with new candles when the old ones have been used up. Having empty candleholders is like empty light sockets—they need to be filled as soon as possible.

Windows are your eyes

The windows are the eyes of your space. If you cannot see clearly around some issue, it is not out of the realm of possibility that you need to wipe your "eyes." Windows not only need to be clean, but any cracked or broken ones need to be repaired. It is not advisable to board up or block any windows for you are, in essence, hampering your clarity. You will not be able to see all aspects of an issue.

If you have a cracked window in your Partnership area, you may want to explore what you or your partner may not be seeing. Repairing broken windows in the Wealth area can assist in clearing up some issues around where your money is going. You may get some in-"sight" by fixing a thermopane window in which the seal has broken, and the glass is fogged. It is more important to fix and repair the original features and structures of your space than to bring in something new. Hanging new curtains on a window with a bullet-hole in it will not alleviate the affects from this violence. The window itself needs to be replaced.

Just as you want to be able to easily see out your windows, you also need some kind of window treatment particularly if your windows are oversized. Curtains, drapes, shades, and blinds are like eyelids on your eyes. They help to protect you from too much light and too much energy coming in. Window treatments can be simple and affordable, yet still be effective. Similar to sunglasses, plain and inexpensive sheers will cut down on the glaring effects of the outside while still enabling you to see.

Windows as your vision

In order for windows to accurately express your vision, they must work. They need to open and close with relative ease. Windows that are painted shut or nailed shut represent a stunted vision that doesn't seem to progress anywhere. If you cannot open your windows, you cannot reach the clarity you want. It is not an issue if a window was never intended to open such as a stationary piece of glass. It is an issue, however, if a window should open but doesn't.

Double-hung windows that allow only half the window area to be open at any one time speaks to a false image being presented to the outside world. The window appears to be other than it is. The message you give is different from what you intend. To remedy this, windows should be the crank-out kind which enable the whole opening to act as a window rather than just part of it. If replacing all of your double-hung windows with the crank-out kind is a financial impossibility, make sure all the mirrors in your house are a clear and clean reflection of you. Likewise, put a round faceted crystal in the Fame and Reputation area of your home to assist in establishing strong and truthful connections to the community.

Windows with stained or etched glass in them enhance the look of your "eyes" to the community. They not only can provide some element of privacy but also add beauty to your surroundings. Windows can also be enhanced by hanging a round faceted crystal in them, particularly if sunlight comes in at certain times of the day. Watching rainbows dance around a room can significantly shift your outlook on life. Windows need to work; they need to be a functioning element in your space; and they need to provide you a clear and accurate outlook on the world.

Mirrors as your reflection

Mirrors are a common adjustment in Feng Shui. They enlarge a space, create a new space, make a wall disappear, move a wall, flatten a wall, or deflect something negative. A mirror does what your intention has created. Mirrors need to be of the highest quality you can afford to buy. Purchasing a cut-rate mirror does not speak well of the sincerity of your intention. If your vision is cloudy and distorted when you look into your mirror, then so is your vision concerning the issue for which the mirror was purchased. If a mirror is chipped or cracked, it needs to be replaced. Do not use tinted mirrors if you want a true and accurate reflection of yourself. Do not use mirror tiles or narrow panels of mirrors on a wall as they cut and slice your reflection, eliminating a cohesive wholeness in your image.

If a mirror is intended to be used for Feng Shui as well as be a functional mirror, it needs to be large enough so that the faces of all the members who will be using the mirror can be seen. If the tallest people can only be seen when bending down, it will bring on headaches and unclear thinking around certain issues. If the shortest people using the mirror cannot see the lower half of their face, in all likelihood, they are not able to speak up or are not being heard when they do speak.

This requires that a large mirror be used if the people sharing it have considerable differences in height. If the mirror is a small decorative one as part of a wall grouping or part of a sconce or light, then the size is not critical because it is not being used as a functional mirror. You want to see your reflection clearly and accurately and with as little distortion as possible. You want to be able to count on its reliability to give you the truth

Mirror placements

There are certain places in Feng Shui when you do not want to incorporate a mirror and certain places where you do. You do not want a mirror at the end of a long hallway because it elongates that hallway even further. You don't want a mirror in a space that's already expansive because it will only increase the perceptual size of the room

You don't want to put a mirror in a place where it reflects a lot of clutter. You, in effect, double your clutter. If you want a mirror in that spot for some reason, then the clutter needs to go.

You do want to incorporate a mirror in a small and dark front entry to help enlarge the space. Having a mirror on one side of a long hallway helps to add width. A mirror facing a window doubles the amount of light in a room. And a mirror hung on a blocking wall makes that obstacle "disappear." It is important to look at exactly what a mirror is reflecting so that, when it doubles something, it's something you want to see twice—a piece of artwork is desirable, but a bookcase in disarray is a problem.

Preparing for a move

Contemplating a move may be one of the most drastic life-changing events that you do in the course of your lifetime. Some people find moving exciting and energizing and don't mind doing it often. Others, who have lived in the same place for years, dread the upheaval and the change. For those in the latter category, there's one thing that can help ease the panic around leaving one house and moving to another. Begin packing and sorting as soon as possible, even if the current house has not yet sold. Taking time to make decisions about what you want to keep and what you want to discard helps maintain your control over the situation. When things have to be thrown into boxes at the last minute, you easily fall into the feeling that things are happening to you without your consent.

Instead, having your belongings sorted and ready to go, labeled, boxed and stacked, helps you loosen your ties to the current space in a pace that you can handle. If a move seems imminent, even if it's a year from now, begin as soon as possible to sort through some things and make decisions about what you want to keep and what you don't. As you begin to "lighten your load" some of the scary elements around changing your environment will lessen. You can take your time, give away those special items you want certain people to have, advertise to sell some things you won't need, and do this process on your terms within your comfort level.

Predecessor information

When shopping for a new home or a new office space, discovering the story of the predecessors helps you make an intelligent decision about whether to move in or not. In a business, you want to occupy a space if the previous tenants were moving to a bigger building because their business had expanded. If the owner of a business was retiring and closing down after many years of success and growth, you will benefit from this space as well.

In purchasing a house, it is beneficial to look for a home where a family has succeeded and expanded so that they need a new place to live. If an elderly couple is moving to a smaller place after raising their family in the house for many years, that, too, is beneficial. If a house has been rental property for some time, you will undoubtedly find a scattered, hectic feeling in the space from the temporary arrangements. When tenants move in and out, there's no commitment or investment to the house. This usually manifests itself in the amount of repairs that need to be done before you can comfortably live there.

If a house has been vacant for at least six months, there's a stagnation that needs to be overcome. If a car is stored for some time, it may not function perfectly right from the start needing some adjustments here and there to get it back to optimum performance. And so it is with a house. It may need to be physically and energetically cleaned in the beginning to get a flow re-established.

If a house was originally a church, a school or an office building before being converted to living spaces, its original intention is very strong and will hold for some time. New occupants need to bless and cleanse the space to eliminate any negativity and to re-adjust the flow of the building's intention.

Predecessor challenges

Even new construction can provide some interesting predecessor issues. If you're building a home in a new development, do some research to find out what the land was originally used for. If structures were torn down and removed in order for the new development to occur, find out as much as you can about the original buildings. It would be important to know if your house was being built on an old prison site or whether it was being built over farmland.

If there was controversy around developing the land into homes, there is a tension that will carry up from the earth and into your life. If the land was undeveloped, but a number of trees had to be removed in order for this development to take place, you want to do some healing work. You can offer tobacco to the earth, spread bird seed or offer a prayer of thanksgiving for the sacrifice the land made in order for you to have your home.

If the builder went bankrupt or had financial difficulties while building your home or any part of the development in which your home is located, make sure your Wealth area in the yard is enhanced in some way to offset the potential difficulties. You may want to install a working light in the back left corner of your lot where your Wealth area is located on the land. A pond could be placed there with clean, flowing water. Being aware of who or what occupied the site upon which you're intending to live is like being aware of who owned the used car you're thinking of buying. You can get a better idea of how the car will run and how well it was taken care of if you can directly speak to the person who's selling it. With your land or home you will have a clearer picture of what will lie ahead if you know what kind of path was made by those who went before you.

Easing predecessor challenges

It is important that you know as much as possible about a piece of property you are considering purchasing. Talk to the neighbors and the owners themselves if feasible. People will leave behind the most recent "scent" of their lives that affects your own experience in the space.

It is not uncommon for patterns to emerge. If the last two couples who lived in the house you're considering ended up in divorce, this presents some challenges in your own marriage or in attracting a partnership to you in the first place. If the previous owners of your house moved because they had filed bankruptcy and needed to get a cheaper house, this, too, adds some financial challenges you might otherwise want to avoid.

If a person has died in the house, this needs to be taken into consideration before buying the property. If the death was peaceful and the process, although emotional, was a conscious, spiritual event for all those involved, then the death is looked upon as more of a transition and is not as problematic. If someone is killed in the house, the space should be blessed and cleared of any remnants from this event. Any kind of abuse—physical, verbal, emotional, sexual—adds to the negativity of a space and needs to be intentionally cleared out. Despite your best intentions, moving into a house with some severe past history can add difficulties and burdens not otherwise encountered. By becoming informed and taking action, you can deflect some problems before they affect your family as well.

Challenges of bunk beds

Bunk beds present some challenges for children who sleep in them. They don't allow enough space for a child to sit straight up which can limit his vision in life and cause some problems in moving ahead. To sleep with a bed or the ceiling within arm's length is too oppressive for a child. It doesn't matter whether the child sleeps on the top bunk or the bottom bunk, there are restrictions either way. The child who sleeps on the bottom bunk has the additional issue of feeling dominated by the child on the top bunk. Likewise, the child on the top bunk may feel insecure about moving too far one way or the other in the narrow bed and falling out.

The most natural way to deal with bunk beds is to take them apart and situate them side-by-side so that each child has a full clear view without the concern of being held down. If the bunk beds cannot be taken apart, then the illusion needs to be created that there's more space between the upper and lower beds and between the upper bed and the ceiling. Placing glow-in-the-dark stars and planets on the ceiling provides the feeling that there's a whole universe above, with endless possibilities.

The child on the bottom also needs to have space created. This can be accomplished with a board that adheres to the underneath side of the top bunk upon which are also placed glow-in-the-dark stars, planets, comets, etc. Again, this can release any confining feelings the bottom child may be experiencing due to the oppression and dominance coming from above. As an option, fabric with cloud images on it can be fastened above the child to provide some expansiveness either on the ceiling or under the upper bunk.

Letting Go

Change is a steady flow

Feng Shui is based on the principle of "flow." This means that nothing stays the same; there's always a constant and perpetual state of flux. Recognizing this change is hard sometimes. There's always the tendency to want things to stay as they are. Since "Feng" means wind and "Shui" means water, the inherent principle of Feng Shui is based on a steady flow of change. Just knowing this can assist in some of the dilemmas that you face during the course of your life's journey.

Being aware that everything changes, you can see that hanging onto something or someone sets you up for disappointment, frustration, and struggle. It is a certainty that events will change, people will change, and circumstances will change. You will change. What may be working now may not be working later. What may be wonderful at this moment in time, may not be so wonderful next week. This is not a fatalistic approach to life, but a conscious and mindful look at the reality of the course of events. Being detached doesn't mean being uninvolved and indifferent. In fact, realizing that all things move on and become something different, you can appreciate what is being experienced now.

Just as "wind" and "water" flows by, the events and the people will never be the same. Even if from the outset things seem the same, they are not. There may be similarities, but it's not the same. Life gets easier and more exhilarating when you can experience this flow and these changes—kind of like "getting in the flow."

Following the flow

When you can see the "flow" of wind and water (Feng Shui) in your space, you recognize what impact it can have in your daily schedule. As in nature, a river will flow and meander to get from one place to the next. The river "surrenders" to the direction of the land, following its shape, moving and zig-zagging as it goes. When your space begins to mirror this "river flow" to you as you incorporate the elements of Feng Shui, you have access to a wonderful, helpful tool that you can use each and every day.

While life gets more and more intense, more frenzied, filled with activities and deadlines, and it's imperative to get everything done in a day, you set goals. You may even write them down so that you don't forget your list of "Things To Do Today." Although beneficial on one level, it can be a source of constant aggravation and frustration if you don't accomplish what you've set out to do that day. Being trained that *doing* is far better than *being*, it is easy to feel like you didn't get anything accomplished. Yet the truth is that you got accomplished all that you needed to get accomplished—you got to the other end of the day. No day is a waste and nothing is a waste of time. It is all part of your river as you zig-zag from moment to moment.

This mind-set requires a surrender mode on your part. It's not that you can't set your goals, but to hope to accomplish each and every goal on your list is probably unrealistic and doesn't leave any room for the unexpected. It's the unexpected that holds the beautiful and poignant moments. Living "in the moment" usually requires that you un-learn the directive about programming certain data, setting your goals, and forging ahead no matter what. When you "live" and incorporate the spirit of Feng Shui, you will find that you accomplish more than you can ever imagine—it just may not be on your list.

Closets are important

Contrary to what you may think, closets hold as much importance in your life as your living room or your bedroom. They are not non-space but can be an asset or a detriment to you depending on their condition. Just as with the rest of your space, your closet needs to "flow." This means that whatever is kept in the closet you can get to easily and you know where things are. Closets are holding places, not junk places. Even though there may be a door on the closet which can be closed to shut out the unsightly random "arrangement" of items, it is still in your space and it is still impacting you in some way.

Having storage space is appropriate. There are times when you need to store things away. You need a place to put winter clothes in the summer and summer clothes in the winter. You need to have a place to put holiday decorations, camping equipment, picnic baskets—things you need only once in a while. The important thing is that you know what you're storing, you're storing what you want, and you can access it painlessly. If it's a monumental project to get to the Valentine decorations, then the closet is not functioning as it should.

Closets need adequate shelving or cupboards. Boxes should be labeled and marked with what's in them. Items need to be stacked so that there's room to get in without having to crawl over other stored items. If there are too many things to be stored in the closet, the first item on the agenda is to take inventory of what you own, and to decide whether it's important to you or not. Often things are stored that no longer serve a purpose. When a closet is jammed full of stuff, the metaphor is that somewhere in your life there's a stagnation and a stuck place that isn't getting loosened. Unload the closet and you'll loosen some stuck aspect of your life.

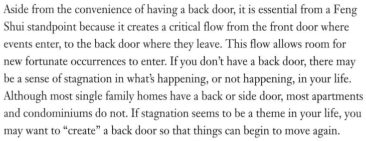

The importance of the back door

Aside from the convenience of having a back door, it is essential from a Feng Shui standpoint because it creates a critical flow from the front door where events enter, to the back door where they leave. This flow allows room for new fortunate occurrences to enter. If you don't have a back door, there may be a sense of stagnation in what's happening, or not happening, in your life. Although most single family homes have a back or side door, most apartments and condominiums do not. If stagnation seems to be a theme in your life, you may want to "create" a back door so that things can begin to move again.

A back door can be "created" by installing a full-length mirror on a wall where a back door would be appropriate if it were physically added (see page 178). A door can artistically be painted on the wall as part of a mural. A piece of fabric can be hung on the wall that is the approximate size of a door. Some clever color patterns can be worked into the wall so that there may be a subtle color shift where you intended a door to be. If life seems to be flowing along rather nicely for you without any sense of stagnation or blockages, then a "back door" may not be needed. If there are large windows in the space, they may be acting as a back door already.

Having a back door in a business is critical to keep the flow of products, services and money coming in and going out. The bigger the back door in a business the better. It allows for more products to get out, and therefore more money to come in the front door. If there is no back door in a business and no hope of having one installed, then painting one on the wall or adding a full-length mirror can ease the situation.

Listening to your home

As you get in touch with your home, you can begin to "listen" to what it needs and to what it's telling you. It will often speak to you in overt ways that are passed off as circumstantial events. A space will tell you when it's time to move, for instance. Major appliances will begin to break down, you may accidentally get locked out of your own house, or a tree may fall on your roof. This is your invitation to move along.

A space can also be very specific about getting rid of something that doesn't belong. A picture will mysteriously fall off the wall, shattering the glass, breaking the frame. Despite your best efforts, an expensive piece of crystal breaks during cleaning. A necklace breaks into a thousand pieces. Your piano does not hold a tune despite repeated tunings by a professional. If, upon reflection, you realize you had some questionable feelings around any of these items, this was your house's way of disposing of some things you couldn't do on your own. If the picture was of your grandmother whom you didn't like, but you felt as though it would be disrespectful to throw it out, and if the piece of crystal was one purchased on your honeymoon, but now you're divorced with no fond memories of that trip, these items would hold some negative energy for you. Your space, in its attempt to take care of you, got rid of some excess baggage.

Reclaiming your energy

"De-cluttering" is the first step in re-claiming your energy and getting out from under feeling overwhelmed. Taking the first step is the hardest. But once you begin to see how exhilarating the process can be you will have no trouble continuing forward. Creating a sense of harmony and peace in your space reflects this same harmony and peace into your life so that you can feel empowered and strong.

First of all, it is helpful to think in small terms when beginning a "de-cluttering" process. If the task seems insurmountable, it is natural for procrastination to kick in. You need to think in terms of small increments of time and small areas of space. If fifteen minutes a day is all you can carve out for yourself, then that is fine. If one part of the dining room table is all you can handle, that, too, is fine. But imagine the cumulative effect if fifteen minutes a day for two weeks was spent organizing an area, then fifteen minutes a day for a month, two months, then twenty-five minutes a day for a month, and on and on. Small steps create big results.

By breaking the task down into small pieces, you can handle the biggest job. Thinking about cleaning out the basement strikes fear into many hearts. But thinking about cleaning one of the shelves under the basement steps isn't so bad. The next day the other shelf; the next day the stuff sitting on the floor under the steps. Often you'll find you get so involved, your fifteen minutes may expand. Done in the spirit of lifting your energy, being grateful for the things you once needed and making room for new events in your life, you'll find yourself surprisingly invigorated and energized. Everything you're getting rid of had a purpose at one time in your life. It is appropriate to be thankful for its use as you send it on its way.

Organizing your storage

"Good" Feng Shui does not mandate throwing out every single thing you're not using this very minute in your life. "Good" Feng Shui does stress the importance in looking at what you own and what you want to keep, however. Chances are you have accumulated more personal possessions than you can use and probably more than you even know you own. A red flag for you to recognize that you've got too many things is if you use the phrase: "I have one of those (a sweater, a can opener, a pencil) but I don't know where it is right now" or "I just saw that the other day but I don't remember where it is." Whether talking about a pair of shoes, a ticket to a basketball game, or a twenty dollar bill, as the owner of your things, you need to know where your things are.

Knowing where your things are requires a system of storage or inventory, so that even if that pair of shoes is packed away for the summer you can easily get to them if needed. In order for this kind of system to happen, you will have to ask some questions about what you own. When was the last time I used this? Do I like this anymore? Do I need this anymore? Will I miss it if it's gone? Asking these questions is how you will determine if you need to bother storing something or move it out permanently.

Not all things are meant to be tossed or given away. You need to store your out-of-season clothes somewhere. You need to be able to put away your holiday decorations. You probably don't want all your photo albums sitting out for anyone to page through. Some things just need to be put away. The key is to know where they are when you need them which means these possessions are in boxes or bags that are labeled for your ease of access. They are stacked so that you can get to them. They are organized so that they are out of the way yet easy to use.

Reclaiming your power

Making decisions about what you own and what you surround yourself with is an empowering and uplifting process. Making sure that all your possessions not only support you but reflect you and your path begins the process of creating a sanctuary. Keeping something that doesn't belong to you, storing other people's stuff indefinitely, holding onto some piece of furniture out of guilt—none of these situations reflects the real you. It doesn't always mean that getting rid of things is easy. There are moments when you may have some second thoughts about what you've released or you may even experience some regrets around its loss. But the main question to ask is if it's serving you any more.

There's a rule of thumb about keeping clothes which says that if you haven't worn them in a year, then you get rid of them. And you know the sense of empowerment and the sense of spaciousness you get after unloading a bunch of old clothes. Even though some of the decisions may not have been easy, once it's done, your sense of relief and energetic enthusiasm outweighs any difficulties in letting things move on. Reclaim some of the power being drained by things that no longer serve you or that are no longer a reflection of your unique and special life.

Older children in your life

When an older child is still living at home or has returned for awhile, place them in a bedroom near the front door so they can find their way out into the world. As long as your intention is to lovingly assist an older child make the transition from your home to their own place, you can set up a bedroom as close to the front door as possible. Those who inhabit the rooms closest to the street are soon gone. If done with compassion and sincerity, you can assist your child in a gentle loving way. Allowing your adult child to inhabit a bedroom near the back of the house assures an extended stay. Although you, as the parent, may not mind this, your adult child will eventually need to become independent.

If your adult child is living in a room near the front door but still continues to stay with no indication of moving in the near future, put a picture of yourself in the bedroom. This will serve as a constant reminder of your presence not only as parent but also as owner of the house.

A teenager living with you can provide many challenges that even Feng Shui cannot adjust! It may seem at times that as you're trying to create a sacred place and a sanctuary for yourself, your teenagers are undermining all attempts by their chaos and disarray. It is no longer appropriate that you as the parent continually clean their rooms or pick up after them, nor is it your responsibility. To offset the turmoil emanating from these bedrooms, there are a few adjustments you can enact. First, keep their doors closed to contain their mess. Secondly, note what space in the home they're occupying (Wealth, Family, Partnership, etc.) and in your own bedroom enhance that area. So if your teenager has a bedroom in the Wealth section of your house and has created a lot of disarray in this area, make some kind of adjustment in the Wealth area of your own bedroom by making sure it's cleaned out and in order.

Making peace with your space

If you haven't made peace with your house before moving out, you will always have some unfinished business. Whether your motive for moving is because you no longer like the house or because you're tired of the upkeep, your move should still be surrounded with gratitude for what the house provided and with anticipation for what lies ahead.

Leaving a house without coming to terms with any negative feelings concerning it will bring those same feelings right along with you into your next house. But this time the issues will be on a bigger scale. This doesn't mean you cannot move or should not move. It means that being clear about why you're moving and attempting to resolve issues before you move will benefit you as well as the next people who buy the house.

If your reason for moving is that the house feels too small and you've gotten sick and tired of having your clothes in piles because there's no room in the closets, you may need to deal with the quantity of things you own and a possible issue with clutter. Otherwise the next house will fill up as well and soon another move will be required.

If your reason for moving is because you've gotten divorced since you moved in, get a clear understanding of what happened in that relationship and what part you played in the split-up. Again, the issue could tag along to the next residence, plaguing you with a similar scenario.

Selling your house

Both realtors and Feng Shui practitioners will tell you to remove all personal things when trying to sell your house. From a Feng Shui viewpoint, you want to begin cutting ties and connections to the house. You don't want anyone else coming in to see that you're still connected in the space, because prospective buyers don't want to evict you from your home. Seeing pictures of you and your children, happy times on vacations, blissful moments at holiday time, wedding pictures and endearing pictures of your dog, prospective buyers not only see but feel the connection you still have with your house. All of these photos need to be removed and carefully packed away for the future home. Likewise, anything with your name on it needs to be removed, such as a personalized welcome mat, a family crest, or your name on the mailbox. It's all part of "neutralizing" the space.

Beginning to de-personalize your house is also very therapeutic for you. It is important that you start to see yourself not living there anymore. It doesn't matter whether you're moving because you need a bigger house, you can afford a better house, or because of a bankruptcy and you can no longer afford the current place; the fact is you are moving. Voluntarily letting go will make your move a lot easier. One piece to successfully moving is to express gratitude to the current house for what it offered you while you were there. It provided you with shelter and safety for a time and gave you a place to operate from. Extending gratitude for these things is a crucial part of your process.

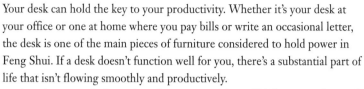

Clearing your desk

Your desk can hold the key to your productivity. Whether it's your desk at your office or one at home where you pay bills or write an occasional letter, the desk is one of the main pieces of furniture considered to hold power in Feng Shui. If a desk doesn't function well for you, there's a substantial part of life that isn't flowing smoothly and productively.

Any time your desk acquires clutter, your vision of life becomes cluttered. The smaller the workspace on the top of your desk, the more limited your creativity. Clearing off the top of the desk and mindfully placing only those things you need or appreciate assists in your feelings of expansion, creativity, and productivity. All of the rest of the items or stacks of papers need to find another place to be—in file drawers, in the trash can, in storage. As you limit the space on the top of your desk, you limit metaphorically the space in your life to introduce the artistry and beauty you need and deserve.

Begin to look at your desk as though a special client was coming to visit you in your office or a very special guest was coming to your home to have you sign important documents. Have only those things on your desk that speak to your sense of style and to your ingenuity. And be selective about how many items you have on your desk—too many things clutter the mind, so remember to go for serenity. By removing everything from your desk, you can clean and dust the top and replace only those items which sing to your heart. Everything else can find a new home.

Creativity

Inspiration at your desk

If you're expecting to be inspired at your desk, surround yourself with inspiration. As you look at all the items and knick knacks on your desk, do any of them give you the uplifting and exhilarating feelings necessary for the creative process? If not, they don't belong on your desk.

Contrary to what you may think, you only need one thing to get the creativity flowing. That one thing can be a picture of a loved one that inspires you to exceed your wildest dreams. It may be a seashell found on a memorable and fabulous vacation. It can be a crystal or stone that holds personal meaning for you. It may be a bell or harmony ball whose sound "takes you away" for a moment. A special flower for a specific project can see you through a few days of creative endeavors.

The point is that whatever you use, you need to be enthralled and enchanted by its very existence. Having all kinds of rocks and stones along with a pine cone or two crowded on one corner crosses over into the arena of clutter. Having a multitude of pictures sitting around on your desktop can also overwhelm instead of inspire. Pick one photo or one stone that holds magic for you at this time and set that up as your wellspring. Later you can exchange the photo for another of your favorites or put a different stone in place of the current one.

The top of your desk holds the key to your creativity. Having an office in the basement or being situated in a cubicle limits your source of creativity. Intentionally placing an object on your desk to afford you limitless possibilities can make the difference between doing your job and being "set on fire."

Placement of your desk

When you're at your desk, your main focus needs to be your work. When you're at a window, your main focus needs to be the view. You cannot do both from the same vantage point. Either the work suffers or you're not fully appreciating the view. Repeatedly people place their desks so that they can work and then look up to gaze at a garden, lake, or some other beautiful and inspiring view. The truth is that you need to get inspired and then take that inspiration to your work space. It's unfair and unrealistic to try to do both at the same time. It's like talking to someone on the phone while balancing your checkbook. Neither activity gets your full attention and neither gets done very well. Some small detail can too easily get lost since your focus is divided.

If you're lucky to have an inspirational view from your office, you can certainly enjoy it from time to time during the day. But this activity needs to be done away from the desk. Find another chair or window-seat from which to soak in the beauty. Appreciate what it brings to you and how it opens your creative soul. Let the view carry you away to vaster realms—as though to rest the mind for a moment. Elicit a feeling of gratitude for the immensity and serenity that the view brings to you. Get inspired. Pay attention to the details. Feel your spirit take on the empowerment of what the view brings. Then carry the inspiration, if only a few steps, to your desk where it can be translated to your work.

Be mindful of how you place your desk in your office. If you're too much "out there" your productivity will suffer. Instead create a small space where you can enjoy being "out" but can return to your desk with renewed interest and vitality. Think of it as taking a walk without leaving your space.

Clearing your countertops

When your countertop becomes so full of what's stored on it that you don't have adequate space to prepare food, your creativity diminishes. *Any* horizontal surface that becomes cluttered cuts down on your vision. A countertop is a horizontal work space. Unless there's something you use every day, i.e., a toaster or blender, it does not deserve to cut into your space. If you've condensed and cleared as much space as possible and still there's no room in the cupboards for some of these things, then enclose them some other way. The vitamins and herbs you take regularly can be put in a basket so that they're all in one place. Or a ceramic container with a lid can hold them. After-school treats can be put in another basket so that boxes of granola bars, potato chips and bags of raisins aren't strewn all over looking for a place to call home.

By condensing a lot of things into one container it makes it easier to keep the countertop clean. You only need to move one thing not twelve smaller items. When cleaning isn't easy, it won't happen very often. Cleaning your countertop shouldn't be a major project, but an easy job that may be done daily if you wish. When there's clutter, the task becomes daunting. But if you can clear your space, you clear your head—and there's plenty of room for new things to come into your life utilizing your creativity and your imagination.

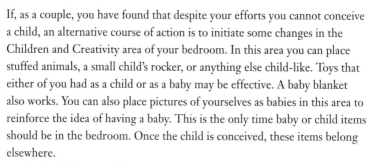

Preparing for conception

If, as a couple, you have found that despite your efforts you cannot conceive a child, an alternative course of action is to initiate some changes in the Children and Creativity area of your bedroom. In this area you can place stuffed animals, a small child's rocker, or anything else child-like. Toys that either of you had as a child or as a baby may be effective. A baby blanket also works. You can also place pictures of yourselves as babies in this area to reinforce the idea of having a baby. This is the only time baby or child items should be in the bedroom. Once the child is conceived, these items belong elsewhere.

In the Children and Creativity area in the main part of the home, an attractive bowl with seeds in it can be strategically placed to represent the conception of the child. A new little "baby" plant can also be considered a representation of new growth. The plant must be tended to on a regular basis and must be removed if there's any sign of decay or wilting. Baby pictures of the two parents can be placed here instead of in the bedroom. Any other pictures of babies would also be appropriate in this area.

In addition, it is best if no remodeling or re-painting is done in the master bedroom while trying to conceive. Very little should be disturbed in the bedroom during this time. Even excessive cleaning can be detrimental to the process, particularly under the bed. If the room becomes too sterile, it is hard for the seed of the child to hang onto anything. If any work is being done during this time, it is suggested you move to a completely different bedroom until all work has been completed.

A blocked entry

If you come face-to-face with a wall or closet when you walk through your front door, you have a blocked entry. In other words, if you have to turn left or right in order to get into the rest of your home or apartment, you are being blocked. It is ideal for you to walk through your front door, into an entry area or foyer and then directly ahead into the living room. When you have to turn to get inside your home due to a wall or obstacle, you may feel blocked in some area of your life. When your vision is cut off physically, it is a metaphor for your vision being cut off on some other level.

If the wall cannot be removed, then the wall needs to become something other than what it is. Hanging a mirror on it provides the illusion of openness and makes a wall "disappear." If a mirror doesn't appeal to you, you can try a print or painting that has a three-dimensional theme that "takes" you into its setting. For instance a landscape with a path running back into the horizon can provide you with the feeling of some depth. A seascape with a broad expanse of the horizon can also give you a sense of space. What you wouldn't want to try to incorporate on this blocking wall is some art that is very aggressive, that comes "forward" to meet you as you enter. A lifesized print of a Siberian tiger is very intimidating as you walk in. Likewise, some modern art that seems to jump off the canvas can be overpowering.

The entrance needs to embrace you and welcome you in. Adequate lighting will help to enhance a blocked entry as well as light-colored walls to give the sense of space and openness.

Holiday intentions

Placing a holiday tree with a Feng Shui intention is an extremely effective way to elicit some changes. The holiday tree includes lights, sparkling ornaments, items that have special memories—all of these things hold a lot of energy. Adding the fiery triangular shape of the tree, you have an immense opportunity to bring about some changes in your life depending on where you position the tree in your house. A tree represents growth (even an artificial tree has the intention of growth); it represents movement with sparkling ornaments and figurines; it represents enlightenment through the use of the lights. An angel on the top provides you with protection. The smell of pine lifts your spirits. Presents under the tree symbolize the exchange of love between you and others. In short, a holiday tree brings with it transformative changes and provides you with dramatic beauty inside your house.

Intentionally setting up your tree in a specific area of your house, although temporary, initiates some changes that might otherwise take a lot longer. Placing it in the Career area of your space will definitely give you a jump-start on some career decisions. Having your tree in the Fame and Reputation area will assist in broadcasting your name out into the community and into the world. If you want some creative spark to kick in, put your tree in the Children and Creativity area of your house. Relationship issues, money issues, family problems can all be addressed simply by being mindful of where you set up the family holiday tree.

Opportunity

A door bell calls in opportunities

The front door acts as a beacon for what you want to bring into your life. Your intention on your door can bring in more money or a new relationship. It can bring you better health or a job more suited to your skills. It can help "en-trance" the right people into your life to help you get what you need or to bring you money. One way the front door can "call in" these people and events is with sound: the doorbell.

Be sure your doorbell works. It's your voice reaching out to "call in" what you want. It's not enough to have an attractive door, you also need some way to sound out the entrance. Even a lighthouse has a foghorn. Not only does the doorbell need to work but you need to like its sound. If the doorbell works, but the sound causes you to jump or it grates on your nerves, change the bell. When the doorbell rings, you want to open your door to opportunities with excitement and anticipation, not with annoyance.

If you don't have a doorbell, attach an autoharp to the front of the door so that whenever it opens you hear its gentle sounds. Or hang a bell on the door knob, attach a door knocker, hang a windchime outside the front door. Any one of these will substitute for a real doorbell. The determining factor for what kind of bell or what kind of chime to get is whether you like it. Just as when the doorbell chimes, when any of these other sound items ring, you want to be delighted to hear its music.

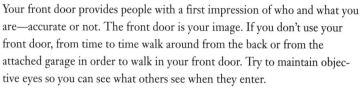

Your front door

Your front door provides people with a first impression of who and what you are—accurate or not. The front door is your image. If you don't use your front door, from time to time walk around from the back or from the attached garage in order to walk in your front door. Try to maintain objective eyes so you can see what others see when they enter.

In Feng Shui the front door is also the entry point for opportunities. It is the only way good fortune and good luck know how to get in. If the door doesn't work very well, opportunities may be passing you by. These opportunities do not know how to get past a door that's wired shut nor do they know how to read a sign that says "Please use side door." If they can't get in the front door, some auspicious events are probably missing in your life.

A front door needs to work smoothly and quietly—any annoying problems and any squeaks need to be remedied. The door knob needs to turn easily. Lights need to work—all burned out bulbs need to be replaced. The coat of paint on the door and on the trim needs to be kept up. The approach should be enticing and free of clutter. Steps should be safe; handrails should be something you can count on. Broken gates need to be repaired. Look at your front door to see what it's telling people about you and to see if you're missing any opportunities.

Red front door for luck

Red front doors hold power and energy according to Chinese Feng Shui. Red is the most auspicious color you can use—it indicates that you're inviting change and new fortuitous events into your life.

It follows that having your front door painted red can have a dramatic effect on the events in your life, not to mention on your neighbors. The idea of a red door holds serious consequences for some people but the red color can be a burgundy or persimmon, purple or mauve. If the idea of a red door cannot be tolerated, a dramatic effect can be accomplished with a green door, or a blue one. The rule is that the door should be a different color from everything else on the house. It should be different from the trim, different from the shingles, different from the shutters.

Whatever color your door becomes, there are two criteria for it to effectively call in all the good fortune you want in your life. First, you need to love the color. It doesn't matter what the neighbors or your mother-in-law say although you may need to make a compromise or two if other family members live in the house with you. Secondly, it needs to be a color that looks good on you so that when you stand by the door you look your best. Check your closet to see if there's any color you wear that you absolutely love and that people regularly notice on you. If your front door makes you smile, you've got it.

Climbing entry stairs

When a home or office is positioned into the side of a hill, it is probable that the front entry is on a lower level, separate from the main part of the space. When you or any guests enter the front door, you have to climb a flight of stairs to get to the living room or reception area. It may be viewed as an "uphill battle" whenever you enter your space. This feature can discourage visitors, opportunities, or auspicious events.

To alleviate a problematic entry such as this, you first need to make the foyer as pleasing and as welcoming as possible. There should be a place for someone to sit and rest before climbing the stairs as well as to put on or take off boots. The lighting should be interesting; any artwork needs to be intriguing; a fountain in the foyer provides an enchanting sound that could resonate all the way up the stairs; a dramatic rug or carpet might tie it all together. Unlike any other circumstance, the foyer in this case has to stand on its own. It is a holding place as well as a transition point for the next occurrence in your space.

To make the stairway seem less of a challenge, make sure there's plenty to look at along the way. Hang pictures that relate by theme or subject matter, or that are by the same artist. You can hang a series of prints so that there is a progression which helps to take someone from the bottom to the top of the stairs. If there's a landing, place a small chair or bench as an optional resting place. The landing can also hold a plant, some lighting in the form of a sconce or a lamp on a table. Because the flight of stairs is imperative in order to find the living room or kitchen, the journey must be pleasant and memorable.

Use your front door

Often due to the position of the garage or the driveway, you may continually enter your space through a secondary door. The side door or back door may be more convenient to use, especially if hauling in bags of groceries or baskets of laundry. Using a secondary door is not problematic unless as a result you never, ever use your front door. Keeping in mind that your front door is the primary place through which good fortune and opportunity will enter into your life, it is highly recommended that you use the front door from time to time.

You need the experience of walking through your front door and entrance on a periodic basis. The front door is your beacon out into the world. It stands for your message to the community. It's advisable to check once in a while if the message you're sending out is still current or if there's anything you'd like to change. If you never use your front door how will you know when a new coat of paint is in order, the doorknob has fallen off or the steps need repair?

A secondary door should not rival the front door for attention. The side or back door should be the same color as the house to help it blend in, unless it's somebody else's front door (i.e. a tenant who lives on the lower level or a business entrance). Even if your friends and family have been "trained" to use the back door, the architectural front door still holds dominance. The side door or back door, despite its amount of usage, is still a secondary door.

Keeping good fortune in your home

When you stand in the front door of your home and you can see straight through to the back door or a back patio door, you have what in Feng Shui is called a front door-back door alignment. This arrangement allows lots of opportunities to come into your life but just as soon as they come in, they're swept out the back door. You have no chance to take advantage of these opportunities; things in your life seem to slip through your fingers. This is the opposite problem of stagnation. You have too much flow happening too quickly.

When your front and back doors are lined up exactly across from each other, you want some kind of barrier between them to slow down what's coming in the front door. You can physically block the view by placing a screen somewhere between the two doors. You can position a large plant or sculptural piece in line with the doors. If you can place a table in this area you could set a floral arrangement on the top of the table to break the visual impact.

If physically there just isn't room to place anything between the front door and the back door, then you can use a diversion to attract your attention to another focal point in the house. If there were a dramatic fountain by the front door as you come in, that may sufficiently break the rapid flow between the front and back doors. If a pedestal with a piece of art on it were positioned near the front door, that can attract your attention. A dramatic and outstanding rug in the front entry will cause your eye to become occupied with it instead of looking out the back door. Any kind of diversionary tactic that catches your eye will break the impact of the alignment between front and back doors, allowing your good luck to come in and stay.

A bathroom overhead

When a bathroom is above a bedroom or an office, it does not bring you the best sense of wholeness or health. In fact this baptism from the bathroom can drain you out and cause an unexplained sense of weariness day after day. Even if the plumbing doesn't run exactly by your bed or the chair you use in the office, it can still impact your productivity and rest.

A small mirror placed on the floor behind the toilet (reflective side down) can separate you from its draining energy. The mirror reflects and separates the energy coming up from the lower level back on itself so that it doesn't mix with the energy in the bathroom. If placing a mirror on the floor is problematic because it may get picked up or moved by cleaning people, small children or even pets, you can affix it to the bottom of the toilet so that it's off the floor but still reflecting down.

If when lying in bed or sitting at your desk, you can still hear the toilet flushing, it is advised to mask this sound with a fountain, a windchime, or some other element that acts as white noise. A radio or stereo can even provide the sound mask you may need. This is true of a toilet anywhere in your space, not just when it's above your bed or desk—if you can hear it flushing, mask the sound.

Bathroom over the front door

If a bathroom is positioned on the second floor so that it is over the front entrance, you can be "flushing away" many opportunities in your life. The front door is the gateway to good luck and good fortune as well as many opportunities that can come along. With the flushing action of the toilet right above the entrance, you may very well be losing out on some chance openings in your career and in your life in general. Even if the bathroom is a small powder room or guest bathroom on the second floor, its impact remains—something is being flushed out of your life.

To counteract such a difficult placement, an interesting solution is to mirror the ceiling of the entrance. In a small entry, it brings a surprise element of space and height as well as separates any difficulties from the toilet above. If that seems a bit radical, a small mirror on the floor behind the toilet (reflective side down) will sufficiently break the connection between the entrance and the bathroom. Alternatively, a small mirror on the ceiling in the front closet can arrange for the needed barrier. In addition, the entrance needs to be attractive, well-lit, and welcoming to whoever enters. A small chime or bell can also be hung in the entrance to transform the energy coming from above.

Sorting the mail

Clutter comes in many forms and shapes. A particularly invasive one that is uninvited is the mail. Piles of it come in each day whether you want it or not. In a very short period of time, stacks of it have taken over unless there's some plan for where it goes and how long it stays.

The first issue is where it initially lands once it gets inside the house. Very simply, you need a "mail spot"—a place where the mail can be seen by everyone concerned and sorted through. This "mail spot" might be a table in the entry or a shelf by the door, but most importantly, it needs to be a consistent place that people can count on. Even if you live alone, a "mail spot" is necessary; otherwise you'll begin to find mail everywhere. The mail does *not* belong on the dining room table, the coffee table, the kitchen counter, the bedroom floor or in the bathroom.

The second issue is sorting through the various elements that come to you through the mail. There's an assumption that you already have a recycling system set up for junk mail and for magazines, and that there's already a special place to put any bills. What's left over is what gets strewn around—a magazine that you want to keep for future reading material, a catalog that you'll want to look through at your leisure, a letter from a friend, a book club promotion. All of these items begin to accumulate into clutter if left on their own.

Finding a creative way to contain those things that require your attention later will help to condense some clutter. An attractive wicker basket, or a wire one, or a box that has a cover can help to store the mail that's at loose ends until you have the time and energy to deal with it. Since it's all in one place, you can access it easily. Once it starts to spill out over the container you know it's time to sort through it to make room for the new things coming into your life.

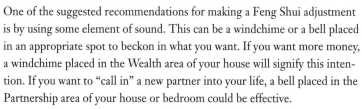

Add sound to your intentions

One of the suggested recommendations for making a Feng Shui adjustment is by using some element of sound. This can be a windchime or a bell placed in an appropriate spot to beckon in what you want. If you want more money, a windchime placed in the Wealth area of your house will signify this intention. If you want to "call in" a new partner into your life, a bell placed in the Partnership area of your house or bedroom could be effective.

Whatever sound vehicle you use, the most important barometer as to its effectiveness is whether or not you like the sound. Even though a windchime or a bell may not be somewhere where it would ring often, if it should ever chime it's critical that the sound be pleasing to you. Select the item with great care, listening to it ring before you buy it and again listening to it in your own space. If there's the slightest annoyance when you hear the chime or bell, return it and get another.

Moving a musical instrument into a particular area reflecting an issue for you can be an effective way to voice your intention. If you can play the instrument, you add your intention as you strum, pluck, or beat. The instrument needs to work even if it doesn't get played very much or at all. If your electronic keyboard is moved to your Career area to assist in a job issue, but it hasn't worked for a couple of years, you need to get it repaired before using it as a Feng Shui adjustment.

Plants represent your intentions

If you want some part of your life to expand and blossom, bring in a plant with these intentions. A healthy plant represents your connection to earth as well as your reach for higher goals. A healthy plant reminds you of the two Feng Shui elements that you always want to incorporate into your space: wind and water. A plant needs both water and fresh air to survive. When using a plant, it is important to be committed to its maintenance. When a plant, which was intended to represent some issue, dies (or begins to die), remove it at once and replace it with a plant that is a little bigger and/or a little more expensive. This emphasizes your strong intention and commitment to the changes you want to bring about. When a plant flourishes and blossoms, enjoy its symbology for your own intention. Taking care of your plant represents the nurturing required to bring about your desired intent.

Placing plants near the front door helps beckon good luck and good fortune. The leaves of plants near the front entrance need to be rounded, soft, smooth, and friendly rather than spiky and pointed. Placing a jade plant near the front door attracts money since its leaves are round like coins. Plants on a desk can symbolize an area where "wind and water" would be welcome. In the back left corner of your desk, a plant can call in more money. In the back right corner it can help to ease difficult partnership issues. Again, it is your job to keep the plant not just alive, but vibrant and lush.

If real plants are problematic because of low-light areas or the care required, you can comfortably use silk plants instead. Silk plants will hold as much intention as real ones. In fact, the benefit of silk plants is that they will never die. However, you do need to clean them off from time to time. Silk or real, plants are a good tool for expanding and bringing to fruition a project, a relationship, a career or any other concern in your life.

Your front door should open wide

Your front door is a symbolic representation of how the world sees you. It is very important that you're clear about what message you're continually sending out to people. The front door sets the intention for the rest of your house. If it's small and dark, it's not conducive to bringing in expansive energy. The message, whether conscious or not, is that you don't want anything or anyone additional in your life. You're content to have opportunities come in small dribbles, if at all.

If your entry is cluttered to the point that the door cannot be opened all the way, you're limiting opportunities available to you. Again the message is that you don't want any good fortune to stop by, or if you do, it needs to be small and controlled. Having good fortune come into your life should be an expansive, exhilarating experience, not a limiting one.

Open your front door wide. Put out the welcome mat. Invite auspicious events into your life. Anything stored behind the front door needs to be put somewhere else, even if it doesn't appear to be impacting the swing of the door. *Nothing* is stored behind the door. Intentionally clear out the space, sweep out the cobwebs and dirt and watch the door welcome good luck and good fortune into your life. Set an intention that whenever the door opens, it will bring in some wonderful event because of its new freedom to swing wide.

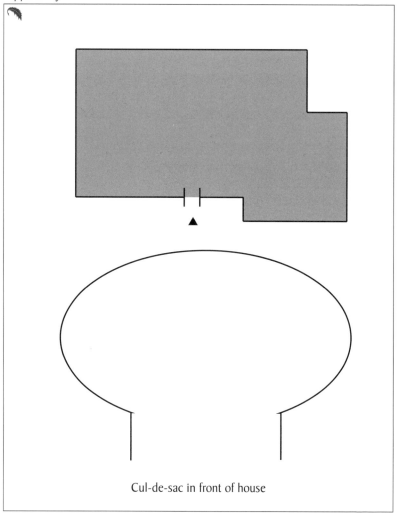

Cul-de-sac in front of house

Cul-de-sac issues

Living at the end of a cul-de-sac does not allow your life to move and flow; instead, it stagnates unless there is some way to cycle the movement around and out again. If you think of the road as a river, when it gets to a wide open space with no outlet, it pools. You can soon be living in front of a swamp. Likewise, a cul-de-sac does not give direction to the flow of traffic. Without a center island to give some meaning to the large open space that comprises a cul-de-sac, there isn't an obvious circular flow. One adjustment is to have a circular island installed in the center so that traffic will understand where to go.

Since the chances of having a center island installed on a city street are minimal, you as a homeowner on a cul-de-sac can help with the flow of the energy as it comes into your area. Hanging a windchime outside your front door will continue the movement. Installing a fountain or windmill can also achieve the idea of motion. Putting up bird houses to attract the activity of the birds will work as well. Your creativity may open up other options that achieve this same affect of circling and flowing in front of your space.

Similarly a circular driveway is always more advantageous than a straight run into the garage. When your driveway comes in straight, traffic comes in and then has to back up to get out. A circular drive in front of the house provides more than one way to get around the property. However, if the driveway circles all the way around the house, you will feel isolated and overwhelmed.

Decorating for holidays

One of the reasons holidays are so magical is because people decorate their homes. Driving down a street where every one of the home owners has strung lights in their yards can conjure up images of being in another world altogether. When your home takes on a new image, you project a different image out into the world. The festive look makes everyone feel spirited. Holiday decorations are a perfect way to begin to understand how Feng Shui works. You use your house to deliver your message to the world. The holidays give you the opportunity to draw attention (good luck and opportunities) to your home.

When you hang a wreath on your front door, you can be using it to attract some new opportunities. Since your opportunities enter your home through your front door only, even a simple wreath will draw attention to the door. If there are lights incorporated into the wreath it attracts even more good luck. In keeping with the tradition of the holidays, for example, tie a red ribbon to it—again increasing its effectiveness for calling in good fortune.

Candles in the windows (electric ones are fine) emphasize your eyes onto the world. When your "eyes" sparkle, people notice. Having your holiday tree near a window so that passers-by can enjoy its beauty also adds fire to your "eyes." Putting up your decorations with intention provides an enchanting and delightful time of year for you and your family, with the health and prosperity you all desire.

Harmony

Feng Shui in the bedroom

To work on a personal intimate relationship, the best room within which to incorporate some Feng Shui adjustments is the master bedroom. When there are relationship issues it is important to keep this room in a balanced and harmonious state. It is imperative that the room reflect both individuals—not a pink lace-filled flower motif where there is no balance of male or yang energy nor a den-like theme with oversized furniture and pictures of wild life reflecting no female or yin energy. The bedroom needs to be a balance of yin and yang even for same-sex relationships.

One way to bring harmony into a bedroom is to incorporate as many round and oval shapes as possible. This can be a round or oval picture, or a picture with round shapes in it. It can mean having round nightstands or some small round pillows on the bed. This feel of harmony can be accomplished with a round or oval rug. Upholstery fabric, wallpaper, bedspread pattern or curtain patterns can incorporate some soft circular shapes. Having some of the furniture at angles to the corner, if size permits, brings a more circular flow into the room instead of having all the furniture up against a wall.

Also using pairs of items emphasizes the idea of a couple—pairs of candles, two chairs, two decorative pillows, two matching light fixtures, a couple of new identical plants. Seeing this "two-ness" reflected in the bedroom emphasizes the idea of an intimate harmony with another person whether you're currently in a relationship or not. If you don't want a personal relationship at the moment, keep the items on a singular basis until ready to add a mate to it and to your life.

Equality in the bedroom

When two people share the same bed, there may be clear messages about the equality of the relationship from certain features in the bedroom. Each side of the bed should have an identical nightstand, with both partners having the ability to turn a light on or off. The underlying theme of which partner is in control exists when only one side is equipped with a lamp. The partner without the lamp has difficulty taking charge of personal bedtime procedures. Either you must both be in bed before the lamp is declared *off*, or one of you walks around the bed to turn off the light, having to get back in the dark without stumbling on something. The other option is that one of you crawl over the other to turn off the light causing disturbance in the process. This sets up tense situations as one partner must give up some control.

For those who are trying to call in a partner but have only one nightstand, the message is pretty clear that there's no room for someone else. If someone else *did* come into your life, they certainly wouldn't have their own lamp! Set it up as though two people are already using the bed, both equally supplied with what they need. It's not very inviting for someone to realize there will have to be either a compromise or a struggle for control in this area.

If one side of the bed is up against a wall, one of the partners has to literally crawl into bed, infringing on the other partner who may already be asleep. Like the nightstand issue, one partner is clearly more dominant and has the upper hand. Even people who do not have a partner are giving a message about the inconvenience there would be if someone dared to come into their lives. Those who don't want a partnership will still do well to have their beds away from the wall to promote a flow of opportunities in their lives and the circulation of good fortune.

Stabilizing your relationship

If a personal relationship seems unstable or unsteady, there are ways you can bring about some security in addition to seeking out a marriage counselor. Even if a relationship is flowing well, it may be wise to anchor it so that during rocky times, there are feelings of certainty and conviction between partners. When anchoring a boat, something heavy is dropped overboard so that the boat won't float off. Likewise, in anchoring a relationship a "heavy" object, either figuratively or literally, is used to keep the partnership on course.

In the Partnership area of your lot a large stone or boulder can be placed with this intention of security. If not a stone, a statue works. An actual anchor may be used to make a literal translation of your intention. Any other building (like a garage, a garden shed, a dog house) speaks to division from the main house, so it does not accomplish what you're looking to do. A tree symbolizes this anchor. Burying a stone or crystal does the same thing. In your home and/or more specifically in your bedroom, another "anchor" can be strategically placed to fulfill the ideas of security, such as a sculptural piece, a large fountain, a heavy piece of furniture (an armoire, an entertainment center, a piano).

A beautiful rose quartz crystal can be placed on your desk in the back right corner signifying a secure and stable relationship. Since pink is the color that the Chinese believe symbolizes this area, the color magnifies your intention. Under your bed in the Partnership corner, place some stabilizing item—a stone or a rose quartz crystal. If there's a possibility someone would move it or take it away during a cleaning frenzy, a smaller stone can be placed between the mattress and the box spring to help take the rockiness out of a relationship.

Working on your partnership

It is not inappropriate to work on partnership issues and difficulties in another part of your house. The obvious area in which to deal with these matters is the master bedroom, but there are plenty of other places where this could be done effectively, either in addition to the master bedroom or instead of the master bedroom. When working on your desk you have an opportunity to place an intention item in the back right corner of your desk. When turning on a stove burner you could use the one in the back right corner for a while. On your dresser you could be certain that the back right corner of this piece of furniture has something representing your partnership—whether it's something you want changed in the current partnership or whether it's about a whole new relationship.

If you have an altar or a special place you might call a shrine, that too could be accessed with the different areas of your life. Intentionally placing a candle in the Partnership area on a regular basis will effect some shifts. Even a small shelf that has only items on it that are yours and that you can move and rearrange as you want could qualify.

Besides putting pairs of things in the Partnership area to represent the number two, or putting a plant representing growth, or flowers meaning beauty, you need to be mindful as to what is already there. Moving clothes hampers from the Partnership area when this is an important issue for you right now would be wise. Likewise, moving wastebaskets would be appropriate if you feel that your partnerships are being recycled more than you like. And, above all, remove any dried flowers in any of the Partnership areas since they are dead and cannot help to promote a blossoming, vital relationship.

Making room for a partner

If you're trying to call in a partner make sure that your current space has room for another person. Despite the objection that if you brought someone else into your life you'd move to a bigger space, it is still a reflection to you and to a prospective partner if you have no room for them. This can mean that there's only one place at the kitchen table to eat—the rest of the table is piled up with newspapers, projects, computer, etc. If someone *were* to come to your space, they readily see that in order to stay for dinner a major overhaul is required. They can see how inconvenient such a visit would be to you. In this case, it doesn't mean you have no room physically, but that you have no room emotionally. The message is loud and clear if you have only one chair by the kitchen table.

You can also ask yourself if there is any room in your closet for someone else's clothes? This may require you to simplify your closets dramatically. Even if, in the end, there is not enough closet space on a physical basis, the metaphor is that you have cleared some old things out and made room for another person. When a new partner moves into another partner's home, there's a critical blending that needs to happen or the new partner will forever feel like a visitor. By beginning to make room for someone to share your life, you not only see that message for yourself on a daily basis but anyone else coming along will pick up on the same message.

Where would a person fit if every square inch of space was taken up with furniture, all wall space was occupied, and each and every closet was jammed full of things? The idea of a new relationship would not feel so overwhelming if there was a possibility of merging two people's lives harmoniously. A new relationship will fit smoothly into your life if you've simplified and made room both on a physical level and on an emotional level.

Calming your child's room

A child's room needs to be as much of a safe haven as yours. In many cases a child's bedroom doubles as a play area and a study area, so keeping it calm can be a challenge. Children get a lot of stimulation throughout the day. Going to their bedrooms should be an enjoyable and nurturing experience. As a parent, you can assist in accomplishing this.

Children's rooms need to be painted in calming colors. There will be plenty of stimulation from other things in the room and from their own daily lives. If the bedroom adds to the excitement of the day, it can set up sleeping problems at night. If a child's favorite color is red, this is definitely a color from which you try to steer them away as a color choice for the walls. Red is stimulating and adds fire to the environment. Some accents of red on pillows and a wallpaper border could be very interesting and effective. The wall colors, however, need to be quiet and serene.

This goes for the sheets and pillowcases as well which these days can often contribute to a child's sleeplessness. Warrior patterns, stampeding horses, ice skating figures all speak to action and excitement. If, however, a child is withdrawn and experiencing depression, brighter colors and more exuberant messages may help to alleviate some of these feelings. Above all, a child needs to be surrounded with messages about rest and safety when in bed. If the child feels safe, the fears that come with childhood will not seem so daunting or so serious.

Cooking with intention

If you want to bring harmony, peace, and balance to your family and to yourself, the surroundings in which you prepare meals must reflect these elements. If the kitchen is cluttered, messy or disorganized, it will be very difficult to bring in the harmony and peace you're looking for. One culprit that surreptitiously undermines these intentions is the refrigerator.

The refrigerator has come to serve two purposes: keep food chilled, or even frozen; and to act as an enormous bulletin board upon which to hang pictures, sayings, drawings, and notes to each other. There's a whole industry that sells refrigerator magnets—magnetic frames in which to put pictures of your favorite people; magnetic puzzles to form interesting sentences which when read seem like they should make sense; and magnetic notepads on which to write memos, reminders and sayings. The refrigerator gets disguised as something other than what it is.

Having so much energy coming off this appliance in a place where a person is trying to create a beautiful yet simple meal provides unneeded stimulation. The "noise" coming from the refrigerator is a source of aggravation and nervous energy which is counter productive to what you're trying to do in the kitchen. To experience the difference between a refrigerator that is "quiet" and one that holds too much clamor, remove everything from the front of it and leave it clear for nine days. After the ninth day replace only those things you feel need to be there so that your concentration doesn't waiver from preparing a healthy, nutritious meal.

Cooking for harmony

If you want mealtime to be a happy occasion, the cook needs to be in a good mood. Whatever the cook's intention while preparing food, that is the tone the meal will take. Unfortunately mealtime has become drudgery and is looked upon as one more thing to do in an already overbooked schedule. It's typically allotted a few rushed moments between other activities. More often than not the entire family isn't present to eat together due to diverse commitments.

If you want more family harmony, someone in the family needs to take the time to cook with that intention in mind. If you want feelings of abundance and prosperity, the cook needs to hold that intention. By cooking with intention, the extra little things get included in the process—candles get lit, special napkins may be used, the freshest foods are included and, above all, enough time is allowed to prepare a decent meal.

As your life speeds up, it's easy to let go of the chance for a family to be together. Even if you live alone, this is the opportunity to treat yourself as you deserve, to nurture and feed both your body and your soul. Cooking is a potential source of facilitating intentional changes in your life.

Preparing meals with mindfulness

If you don't personally know who cooked your food for you, it will probably not be prepared with your best interest in mind. The problem with processed foods and fast-food restaurants is that the cook doesn't know the customer. Low pay and unfortunate working conditions doesn't inspire someone to cook with love and compassion. In the case of processed food there may not even *be* a human cook. When there's no healthy intention put into your food, it is difficult for you to extract healthy nutrition from it.

When food comes from packages, the energy has usually been destroyed during the processing of it. Yet the pace of life being what it is, it may not be possible to put this amount of consideration and mindfulness into preparing meals on a regular basis. Cooking with intention just once a week will make a significant change in your life. Holding your highest good as your intention while steaming fresh peas or preparing fresh strawberries for dessert will not only change the subtle energy of these foods, but they'll also taste better!

Peaceful meals

If you want peaceful, happy mealtimes, make sure your kitchen table exudes this kind of energy. A table piled full of the day's activities creates chaos which carries over into the meals. A kitchen table needs to be clutter-free and clean. A beautiful centerpiece or a pair of simple candles will add an aesthetic touch. There should be an even number of chairs around the table making sure that the home owners or the main residents have chairs that face the entrance to the kitchen. Even if there's only one person living in the space, it is important to have at least two chairs around the table, particularly if you're trying to draw in a personal relationship.

Keeping the table simple and clear helps alleviate feelings of being crowded if the eating area is small. It is important to look at the European cultures to realize that mealtime is an event. There's plenty of time allotted during the day for a noon meal, and dinners are usually long and leisurely, occurring around 9:00 PM. In some Asian traditions, the only talk allowed at the table is discussion about the food that's being consumed—how delicious it is, what it tastes like, how grateful everyone is to the cook who prepared such a delectable feast. There are no arguments about politics, school grades, teen-age behavior, or finances. The meal is peaceful and relaxing—something everyone looks forward to.

Resolve the unresolved

You don't want to move from a home just to "get away" from something unpleasant. You want to move to another phase of your life with anticipation and excitement. It's one thing to close a chapter on your life—it's another to leave in mid-sentence. Any unresolved issues need to be faced directly so you can eventually walk away cleanly, without any regrets. If you can't stand to drive by a home you used to live in, you have unfinished business from this part of your life. You can still come to terms and heal from the experiences there but you need to be willing to take the time and exert the energy.

Leaving behind some unsettled issues is similar to leaving your trash behind at a camp-site. Nobody wants to pick up after you so you have to clean up your own mess. Whether you're living there or not you can cut the ties that still hold you to an old house. Only you can answer exactly why there are still feelings around the place. Maybe there needs to be some forgiveness expressed towards another person or persons, towards the house itself, towards yourself. Guilt may be tied up into all of this—guilt around leaving, maybe around your behavior, your actions or inaction.

The goal you want to strive for is to have accepting feelings and possibly warm memories toward the house. Above all you do not want to leave a home without closure. Otherwise, you will be moving some unexpected guests with you to reappear in a new disguise but with a familiar air.

Wealth

Keep your money flowing

A back door in the Wealth area of your space leads to money quickly flowing out of your life. You need a back door, not only from a fire and safety standpoint but also because it represents indirect opportunities coming into your life. Metaphorically it also symbolizes the cyclic part of nature which Feng Shui uses as its model—money comes in through the front door and needs to go out a back or side door. But when this second door is in the Wealth area, too much money escapes. Aside from moving the back door, you can adjust this situation with several options.

If your door is in the Wealth area of your space (home or business), you can hang a chime either inside or outside the back door. This chime's "job" is to call back your money so it's not lost forever. The chime helps your wealth cycle through the universe and come back through your front door. Instead of a chime, you might hang a bell on the door knob, either inside or outside. You can also hang a bamboo flute horizontally over the inside of the back door with the mouthpiece pointing toward the main part of the house. Bamboo flutes are used for protection. In this case, you're protecting your money.

Hanging a round faceted crystal in a window near the back door can, at certain times of the day, cause a richness of rainbows to fill your space. If there is no window, a crystal can be hung on the inside but far enough or high enough from the door so that it doesn't bang every time the door is opened. Since purple or lavender are the colors that represent wealth in Feng Shui, you can paint the inside of your back door in one of these colors. Or, you can hang something purple or lavender on the inside of the back door—a purple curtain, lavender fringe on a curtain, or purple tiles. Whatever adjustment you feel represents your intention to maintain the cycle of money through your life, it will soften the effects of a back door in Wealth.

Wealth on your desk

Paying attention to what is in the Wealth area of your desk can exemplify what money means to you. If money is an issue in your life, look at this area to see what is occurring. Use the desk that is considered your main one—any other computer desk or side secretary desks would be secondary.

In coming to terms with this particular corner of your life, the first recommendation is to clear off everything in the Wealth area. This is an area that mirrors abundance and prosperity. You need to ask yourself if the back left corner of your desk reflects that same message. All "dead" files, old coffee cups, wilted flowers and pending projects should be dealt with and either tossed or stored. By clearing everything off you can replace *only* what speaks to you of being prosperous. This might take the form of flowers, a plant, a small fountain, a candle, an aromatherapy diffuser, or whatever else causes you to feel "rich." There are lots of ways to feel wealthy so it doesn't necessarily follow that you place something overly expensive in this corner. Likewise, it also doesn't mean that you plunk down some used broken item you got at a garage sale because it's all you can afford. Remember, the message is about prosperity.

A brass bell is a very traditional Feng Shui adjustment in the Wealth corner of the desk. Your intention is to "call in" abundance. When you receive any money you put it under the bell with gratitude until you deposit it or spend it. It's not even important that you ring the bell when placing or removing the money although doing so is a very auditory reminder of your intention. If you use a bell, however, you still want to make sure you enjoy its sound because, rung or not, it becomes your voice to the universe regarding your money preferences.

Fountains keep things flowing

It was believed by the Chinese that if you had water on your land, you could grow rice and therefore you would have money. Having water on your property is still considered auspicious. Many people buy a secondary home or a retirement home on a lake to be near this element. But there are other ways of bringing water into your life besides living on a lake, a river, or the ocean. One way is with fountains.

Fountains not only exhibit the element of water but the element of motion as well. The sounds of a fountain cause most people to relax as though remembering a simpler time when they relaxed by a waterfall. Bringing the sound of water into your space brings a calming, peaceful serenity which can enhance your productivity and creativity. Adding its connection to money, a fountain can be a very favorable item to have. Fountains need to be working, flowing well, clean, and maintained. If purchased with the idea of having more money in your life, keeping it operating smoothly is critical.

If a fountain is placed in the Wealth area of your space or of your room, it can add to the intention of drawing in money. Every time you turn on your fountain you can be turning on the intention for a bigger and better flow of money. It is imperative that if the motor begins to malfunction you get it fixed or replaced immediately. If the water begins to look a little murky, change it at once. A fountain requires maintenance and care which reinforces your money intention each time you have to tend to some detail on it. It is better to remove a fountain that doesn't work than to leave it there indefinitely. If a fountain is left to go stagnant or is in disrepair, it's difficult to keep the flow of money coming in.

Aquariums provide opportunities

The "flow" of money can come into your life as the result of installing an aquarium. Aquariums are particularly powerful since they hold the element of water and they contain the elements of motion and life. On the other hand, they are very labor-intensive, requiring an owner to see to their needs every day on a long-term basis. This is a commitment that should be considered before investing in an aquarium since ignoring something that needs care is at cross purposes to your original intention.

An aquarium, however, can provide an incredible amount of beauty and serenity. It is a great reminder of the cycles of nature. Having an aquarium in your space whether it's your living room, a den or a reception area causes those who come into visual contact with it to see and feel its motion and to slow the pace a notch or two. Even a small bowl with a couple of gold fish provides an opportunity to unwind.

An aquarium provides you with an opportunity to remove yourself from your daily life and to immerse yourself into another "world" which is less hectic and busy. It enables you to see the value of life and to appreciate the exquisite beauty that you can create in an aquarium. It is very auspicious to have nine fish in an aquarium if size permits—either eight black and one red, or eight red and one black. Making the aquarium "world" as beautiful as possible enhances its power. Positioning it in the Wealth area of a room, office or business taps into the source of wealth to help bring more money into your life. It is up to you to take care of the fish!

Water brings in wealth

Any time water can be incorporated into your space it will help to enhance your chances of money flowing freely. When you live with moving, clean water in front of your house, you have access to a flow of money. In order to capitalize on the water on or near your property, position a mirror inside your house so that it can reflect this flowing water and bring it into your living space. It's as though you have "virtual water" in your space. It's better than a picture since the mirror will reflect the movements, the waves, the ducks or birds flying around it, the reeds waving. A mini-version of a lake has been captured on your wall for your enjoyment as well as to help bring water/money into your life.

If you are not fortunate enough to have flowing water in front of your house, you can install a birdbath. By size standards this seems like a huge compromise, but the immense activity of the birds due to the water is not to be overlooked. Birds bring with them good luck and good fortune. Also due to the maintenance that you have with a birdbath, you become more engaged with your intention than you would with a lake scene. Like a fountain or an aquarium, a birdbath needs to have a constant supply of clean water. Letting it dry up is like letting your financial resources "dry up." Placing the birdbath in the back left corner of your lot in the Wealth area is one auspicious place to have it. Setting it in front of your house is also another good place since it can represent the river flowing by the front of your house. As with the lake you can have a mirror that reflects the birdbath and its surroundings back into your house to double its effect.

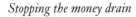

Stopping the money drain

A toilet in the center of your money area will easily take your money away with each flush. As the toilet creates a large vortex of swirling energy, you can watch your finances swirl out of your life as well. Water is directly related to money—if you have one, you'll have the other. When water leaves your space with such great force and impact, your money can leave with it as well.

Keeping the lid of the toilet down when not in use is one way to counteract this "drain" of money. Keeping the door closed to the bathroom is also effective. Having a mirror on the outside of the door also adds to the deflection of this money drain. Or place a small round mirror on the ceiling above the toilet (reflective side down) to "reverse" the action of the drain so that your money will remain in your home. All of these Feng Shui adjustments will help to counteract money leaving your house through the toilet. If, while doing these adjustments, the bathroom sink has a slow leak, your money is still finding a way to slip out. All leaks and drips need to be addressed as soon as possible.

Having the bathroom, even a small one, attractive and well-lit is important to keep your wealth intact. Placing a small green plant on the top of the toilet tank can represent the growth and blossoming of your finances. A small arrangement of silk flowers will also give this message. Although your bathroom is a private room, many people who come to your house are apt to use it. Making it as beautiful and charming as possible speaks to your sense of wealth and success.

Detachment from your money

The attitude with which you spend money is similar to the attitude with which you may work out or the attitude with which you clean your house. Any of those activities can be drudgery, even painful, unless done with a different perspective. For so many people, spending money or paying bills is done with hesitation and begrudgingly. These activities should be done in a state of gratitude, not only for what you've received in return for the money, but also for having enough money in the first place to make this transaction happen.

Getting into the flow of money will enable you to understand how the process must work in order to bring in more money. To help you give out your hard-earned money to the various services you've contracted and purchases you've made, you have to let go of the idea it's your hard-earned money. It's money, not yours or anyone elses. If you've ever travelled in a foreign country you've probably experienced the weird sensation of spending their currency. It almost becomes like "play money" with its different colors, sizes, and denominations—you certainly don't have as much attachment to it as you do when you look at our familiar presidents' faces in the recognizable green color. This is not a pitch to spend money as though it has no value, but to spend money without the attachment. When you're detached you can pay your bills or purchase what's needed knowing that more money will come in to replace what was spent.

Give a little extra

One way to detach from the idea that you own your money is to add something specifically yours with the payment. For example, you can pay all your bills in red envelopes, or in an assortment of brightly colored envelopes. In a creative surge, you can make some envelopes out of homemade paper. Find some stickers that represent something you stand for, your favorite color, your favorite animal, a saying you like—fix one to each of the envelopes going out with a payment. Buy postage stamps that are out of the ordinary. When paying for your next hair cut, put the money in an envelope with a thank-you note to your stylist for good work. Pay a compliment to the check-out clerk. On another level, at least bless each of the payments leaving your domain. Whatever you do, you want to add value to the payment so that it becomes more than what it really is. This is the part that comes from *you*—the money is only moving through the exchange of hands as it was intended.

It is imperative that you come from a place of compassion and concern in your heart. And it is important that your intention be to not only pay the bill, but to pay *more* in this subtle way. It's as if you're saying that you haven't paid enough for whatever you're purchasing and because of your abundance and flow of prosperity, you want to pay an additional amount. Whether it's a special edition of a postage stamp or a simple compliment about a clerk's sweater, you have enhanced the exchange of money and opened the door to receiving more.

Buy the best

Money is not the root of all evil, contrary to what some people think. Money can be beneficial on many levels not only to you but to those who can benefit from your wealth. If money is hoarded with little intention of sharing, then it becomes ineffective to the common good. If money is given away with little regard for necessary provisions you may need in your life, money again becomes ineffective to the common good. Like the flow of wind and water in Feng Shui, money needs to circulate through your life. If you want more money, you need to allow it to leave, so that more will come in.

If monetary decisions are made with the intention that you'll buy the cheapest because that's all you can afford and that's all you're worth, that's all you'll *ever* be able to afford. Using good judgment, it is not always in your best interest to buy the lowest priced items. In fact, the cheapest items reflect to you continually the message about your self-worth. If your intention is to have more money in your life, allow it to become honoring. Allow it to purchase for you the best you can possibly afford. If you buy a pair of leather boots which were more than you would normally spend, but you loved them, they felt good on you, they looked good on you, then those are the boots for you. If you had sacrificed and, instead, went to a discount store to buy some imitation leather boots, not only would you have been reminded every time you wore them that this was all you could afford and this was all you were worth, but they will probably hold up only half as long as the leather boots.

Quality in Feng Shui is about owning the best things possible within your budget. Owning less things will make buying the best a reality. If you spend your energy (money) on only those items that are meaningful and of the highest quality for you, your life will become abundant and full of prosperity in no time.

Trusting the flow of money

If you keep an item "just in case" you may need it later, you're setting yourself up for some financial challenges. If you keep something with the thought that *later* (next month, next year, after weight has been lost, after the kids leave, after you retire, next time you go to Hawaii, next time there's a costume party, etc., etc.) you may have a use for it, you're making a proclamation and an affirmation that you will not have the money to buy what you need when you need it. If this is your mindset, this affirmation of "not having enough" will surely program itself into your life. Lo and behold, your prophecy has been fulfilled: you won't have enough when you want it.

Feng Shui is about flow. Flow implies movement—up and down, back and forth, in and out. What you let go of now will be able to flow back to you when you need it. Your trust in having "enough" to get what you need at a later date will manifest the resources. Letting something go out of your life is a sure invitation for it to come back in when appropriate.

Besides "just in case" items take up precious space and drain precious energy from you. Having a whole basement of "just in case" things sets up the foundation of your life with concern about having enough money or energy later. Your basement supports your whole house; your house reflects your life. Obviously what you keep in your basement is of ultimate concern. Furthermore those "just in case" items are hardly ever used anyway because when you want them chances are you won't be able to find them. Or if you find them you realize that your recollection of how great this item was is mistaken. It's not as perfect as you remembered, or it's not the quality you remembered, or it's simply out of date and a new one would be much better. Don't waste time (or energy) on an item that has no value to you today.

Paying your bills with gratitude

How you care for your bills will determine the ease with which they get paid. Bills are almost always for services you have already used. A credit card bill is for things you've already purchased, used, or worn. A phone bill includes long distance charges for people to whom you've spoken. A car loan is for a car you're using. It goes without saying that there should be an element of gratitude for these bills since someone somewhere without personally knowing you has trusted that you will pay the bill. Someone has decided that you're an honorable person with the integrity required to make good on your promises.

Where and how you handle these reminders of your good reputation is critical in enhancing the flow of money. If bills become a constant source of irritation, you're defeating any attempts to bring the "wind and water" flow of Feng Shui into your life. Money needs to go out in order for it to return. Breath needs to go out in order to make room for breath to come in. Treating bills like the gift they are and keeping them in a place where you honor them for safekeeping begins to change a narrow and limiting paradigm we have about bills.

If you keep them in a special box or held together with a ribbon, it's a reminder to you of their importance. They do not belong on the top of your desk due to their personal nature, so store them in a drawer or a file cabinet. When you go to pay a bill, bring them out as though you're handling letters from a dear friend. By stacking them in order in which they're due for payment, you don't have to go through each and every one to see what's due when. By managing your bills, not only will they get paid on time, but there's the added benefit of beginning to view them as tokens of your honorable integrity. It's your chance to give back for what you've already received and make room for more money.

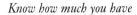

Know how much you have

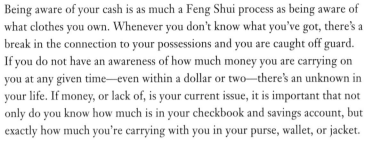

Being aware of your cash is as much a Feng Shui process as being aware of what clothes you own. Whenever you don't know what you've got, there's a break in the connection to your possessions and you are caught off guard. If you do not have an awareness of how much money you are carrying on you at any given time—even within a dollar or two—there's an unknown in your life. If money, or lack of, is your current issue, it is important that not only do you know how much is in your checkbook and savings account, but exactly how much you're carrying with you in your purse, wallet, or jacket.

If money is found here and there—crumpled dollar bills in the bottom of your purse, coins in a dresser drawer, a $20 bill shows up in the pocket of a suit you haven't worn since last winter—there's an indication of not being fully aware of your cash flow. All of the money you carry with you, down to the last penny, needs to be accounted for. Spending becomes careless without a definite awareness on what you can afford and what you can't.

It will be important for you to gather all your money in one place—maybe a wallet—count what you have and always have some connection to how much is in there. Getting caught short at a check-out counter or at a gas station is a clear indication that you do not know what you own and have not bothered to take stock. Your money is an important source of energy that needs to be treated respectfully. The least you can do is keep track of how much of this energy you have with you.

The nine-day cash experiment

One way to get in touch with your money and to appreciate its value is to pay cash for everything for nine days—groceries, gas, postage, furniture. Actual money hardly ever exchanges anyone's hands anymore. Money has taken the form of a check or a plastic card. This distance makes it easy to spend and over spend. Automatic withdrawal, although a convenience, contributes to this gap. But if just once you cash a paycheck or a commission check taking as much money as you'll need without having to write a check of use a credit card, for a span of time, you will actually see your money, handle it, and count it out. Doing the experiment for nine days will add to its impact. In Feng Shui, the number nine is a powerful culminating number and holds a strength and intensity that other numbers do not.

If all your money is in the form of cash, you'll know when it's time to stop spending because your wallet will be empty. You'll have had a direct personal experience of spending it and know what you spent it on. You'll see it exchange hands for each purchase you make. It may even cause you to think twice about buying something knowing the money that will be needed to buy it will be used up that much more quickly. It doesn't take a rocket scientist to calculate how many work hours it takes to earn the amount of money needed for a particular purchase. Paying in cash helps slow down the spontaneous shopping sprees.

If at the end of the nine days or at the end of your experiment with money, you have nothing left over, you take stock of where it went and whether it was well-spent. Money is meant to be a friend and an ally, but like your pet dog, if left out of control and untrained, it becomes more of a burden in your life than a pleasure.

Tending the stove

Whether you cook or not, your stove represents the flow of energy in your life. This flow takes the obvious form of physical nurturing, feeding both body and soul. It also represents the financial flow you're currently experiencing—or lack of flow. The stove is the center of warmth, the place where people gather and where food is prepared. If the stove doesn't work, there's a critical life element that's not working either. It doesn't matter if you don't cook much or if you cook at all; it does matter that the stove be functioning properly regardless of the use it gets. All the burners need to be operable and clean. They are like the cylinders in a car—when any one of them doesn't work or is not burning smoothly, you don't have as much "horse-power."

Keeping the top of the stove clean may seem obvious but often in the bustle of daily activities it doesn't get the attention it deserves. Cleaning the burners doesn't have to be a dreaded chore every month or even every six months if they are kept cleaned and wiped up on a regular basis. The intention isn't to create another big project to fill your time, but to realize that staying on top of the issue takes only moments. With your intention, the burners bring in abundance on many levels—physical health, financial success, and supportive people.

Money in the kitchen

Your financial situation can improve by realizing the importance of the burners on your stove. The burners are part of a prosperity cycle that begins with the idea that even the poorest of people would gather around this fire to fix whatever meagre food had been acquired. The intention was that the food would sustain a person's energy so that the next day more money could be earned to acquire more food. This, too, would be prepared over the fire, eaten with the idea of being able to maintain the energy to earn a little more money and therefore acquire a little more food. This food would again be eaten, energy increased, additional money earned, and so on.

Being mindful of the flow of money as you prepare food for your family greatly increases your prosperity. It's intention is to sustain and nurture your body so that your creativity and productivity is enhanced, and therefore your earning power. Without this intention, a meal is simply a point in the day when everybody chews and digests food—sometimes together and sometimes separately. Even if the stove is not involved in the preparation of a meal, it's the activity of putting a meal together that can enhance the abundance of body, mind, and spirit.

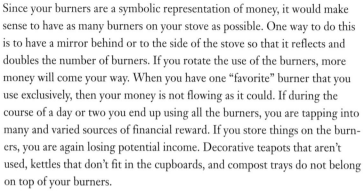

Money and your burners

Since your burners are a symbolic representation of money, it would make sense to have as many burners on your stove as possible. One way to do this is to have a mirror behind or to the side of the stove so that it reflects and doubles the number of burners. If you rotate the use of the burners, more money will come your way. When you have one "favorite" burner that you use exclusively, then your money is not flowing as it could. If during the course of a day or two you end up using all the burners, you are tapping into many and varied sources of financial reward. If you store things on the burners, you are again losing potential income. Decorative teapots that aren't used, kettles that don't fit in the cupboards, and compost trays do not belong on top of your burners.

To emphasize the importance that burners play in acquiring money, you can turn on all the burners once a day during critical financial crises, seeing your money energy flowing into your life. Do this once a day until the crisis has passed. Then maintain the burners, keeping them in good working order and clean with the stove-top uncluttered. Whether you have an electric stove or a gas range, these principles still apply. Having a gas range, however, is preferred because of the element of fire with which you can cook your food.

Placing your wastebasket

If your wastebasket is in the Wealth area of the room, you may be throwing out your money. If your wastebasket is there, you may be experiencing some financial stress. The simplest thing to do is to move the wastebasket to another part of the room so that you don't throw out your money when you empty the basket.

If there's no other convenient place for the trash then make sure the wastebasket doesn't get to be over-flowing, with garbage falling onto the floor. Make sure you empty it regularly. Enforce the intention of throwing out only those things which you no longer need in your life, but keeping those things (like money) that you do want. If the wastebasket has to be in the Wealth corner, it would help if it were aesthetically pleasing and decorative. Painting it or wrapping a ribbon around it can soften the loss of money. Having a cover or lid on it will also counteract the loss. Having some purple (the color for money) on it can be another option if it works into your design scheme.

The color purple

The color purple can enhance money coming into your life. Using purple or a variation of purple in the back left corner of your home, office, or bedroom, as well as on your desk, adds to the adjustment of bringing in more money. A purple vase filled with flowers is one option for your desk or a clear vase with purple flowers will also work. An amethyst stone can be set on your desk for money. A purple candle may be burning in the Wealth area of your bedroom. Lavender pillows can be used on a sofa that's in the Wealth area of your home. Painting a wall or two in that area with just a drop of purple coloring mixed in the paint will enhance your wealth.

There is always the option of wearing purple if it's a color that looks good on you. Don't wear something you wouldn't ordinarily wear or that you know washes you out or makes you look particularly bad just because it's a Feng Shui adjustment. Each adjustment made with an intention has to involve something you are invested in—if you're indifferent about an object or actually don't even like it, your intention will find it very hard to bring in what you want. Remember, it is your intention that makes this work. If you still want to wear purple but it's not the most flattering color, wear it under your clothes. Or wear a very small amount of it—an amethyst pin or a small wash of purple in a silk scarf.

Likewise, don't paint your bedroom a lavender even if it's in the Wealth area of your home if lavender doesn't look good on you. If every time you look in the mirror you see yourself surrounded by a color that makes your skin look a light shade of green, lavender walls will not be helpful. If you still want to use that color, you can find less dramatic ways of bringing a purple variation into the Wealth area. In order to feel abundant you need to feel good.

Sanctuary

Creating sacredness

The ultimate purpose of Feng Shui is to enable you to find an inner sacred space—an inner sanctuary you can access whenever you want. To assist you in doing this, however, you create sacred space on the exterior to help that journey within. Finding sacredness in your environment is really all about the search for wholeness, for the integration of mind and body, spirit and matter. Finding sacredness in your environment nourishes the soul, fosters inspiration, and renewal.

Sacredness is not reserved for places like Chartres Cathedral or the power spots in Sedona, Arizona, or even Stonehenge in England. Sacredness can be found in your own immediate life and in your own house. You need a sacred space where you can feel whole and safe. This may be as simple as a shelf in the corner of a room or an altar. It may be one room set aside for study, reading and meditation. It may be a garden. Ideally your entire house could be transformed into a temple. With the right intention, any place can be sanctified. You can make your space sacred not by controlling it or manipulating it, but by listening to it and working with it.

Listening to a space requires that the space be left "quiet" for a while— with little or nothing to disrupt what it's trying to say to you. As you listen, you'll begin to hear what needs to happen or what elements need to be added to make the space a sanctuary. These "messages" may direct you to bring in a pillow, add a plant, bring in fresh flowers, put a favorite rug on the floor, hang a tapestry. This listening process may take two weeks, two months or a year. But as you begin to feel the harmony between the inner and outer, it will bring you into your own sacred space. An exterior space that has become sacred knows what's best for you and can help you find your own inner sanctuary.

Designing your bedroom

When redesigning or first conceptualizing a master bedroom, think of the sweetness with which you'd design a nursery. There are just some things you don't put in your bedroom—like a television, a computer, your ironing board, a stair-master, a gun collection, piles of old clothes. Instead of nurturing your own inner child by providing a secure and safe space, you set up challenges to deny yourself the opportunity to grow your creativity and sense of well-being. Put only those things in your bedroom which speak to your comfort and safety on an adult level.

If you're trying to call in a partner or resolve some partnership issues, you don't want to have your bedroom overrun with stuffed animals depicting a younger, more innocent time in your life. As a child, having stuffed animals in your bedroom is appropriate. As an adult, however, you do not want to be a child in your own bedroom. Likewise having pictures of yourself as a baby or as a little kid in your bedroom depicts you as a child—again not appropriate for an adult's bedroom.

Your bedroom is meant to be just that—a room for your bed, not a workout space, a place of business or an entertainment hub. Your bedroom is for intimacy, sleep, and getting undressed. Period. Anything that speaks to other activities needs to find a new "home" or at least be screened off at night so its impact isn't as direct. When you capture a sweetness and a serenity in your bedroom, you feel safe and assure yourself of a good night's sleep whether sleeping alone or with someone else.

Making your bed

A very simple two-minute activity that can help you feel like you have your life under control, and that, despite the outward appearance of chaos, you are not as scattered as you think, is to make the bed each morning. This is not meant to be a retentive project that reminds you of your mother's orders when you were a child, but instead a mini-ritual that provides you with a moment or two of quiet. Making the bed can be a shared ritual with your partner as you tuck away the memories of the night together. You can begin your day with a small token of mastery which will carry you forward into other realms. Doing something proactively sets a pattern for other proactive behavior in different situations.

Not only will such a small act assist in giving you a handle on daily affairs, but it helps to unclutter your space. Returning at the end of a long and full day to see the peaceful, simplisitic setting of your bed, covers folded carefully, pillows placed just right, can mirror to you the peace and simplicity you want in your life. It can be a reminder of the sanctuary you've created in your bedroom where all things are quiet, safe, and certain. As busy as life can be sometimes, some days making the bed will be about all that helps to center you!

Appreciating emptiness

It is a mistaken belief that if a corner has nothing in it or a table doesn't have at least a dozen items or knickknacks displayed on it, a space will look too bare. Quite the contrary, an empty corner is a "quiet" corner; it can breathe and allow something new to enter into your life. Sometimes when a corner has been cleared out it is appropriate to leave it open for a while. Soon enough you will know what, if anything, belongs there.

Likewise the top of a shelf or the fireplace mantel or the top of an end-table feels "empty" without a lot of things on it—pictures, mementos, whatever. But as an experiment, try leaving one horizontal surface completely clear for nine days and see if you've come to appreciate the serenity it exudes. Not every surface has to be occupied or every corner filled to make a space "work." Just as in music there are rests when the melody stops or breaks momentarily, just as in your own lives you need down-time to rest from your normal daily activities, so does your space need some contrasting areas to complement the other items you own.

The impact of your car

Your car can have as much influence on your life as your home or office. Many people spend a lot of time in cars, either commuting to and from work, or as a sales person out on the road. The state of your automobile can impact dramatically the state of your well-being and productivity.

The automobile has taken on monumental importance. Many people have attached garages for the convenience of getting to the car when they need to. Having this attached garage usually affects how you enter your home—with an attached garage you hardly ever enter through your own front door. And now more and more you can see houses being built with the garage projecting forward out in front of the house, distracting the energy from getting to the front door. When the garage is the first thing someone sees upon arriving at your house, this architectural feature makes a blatant statement about what's important in your life. This message is clearly that your life revolves around your car—you live in your car—your car is home.

Since most people can't live without this mode of transportation, it's important to examine this mobile space to see how it can impact your life. Just like your home or office, the first question to ask yourself addresses the problem of clutter. Getting into a car with old coffee cups, left-overs from yesterday's lunch, and a pile of old newspapers doesn't provide inspiration. In fact, it drains your energy, and it can be a source of annoyance. It exacerbates the aggravation of driving which is aggravating enough as it is. Just as you clean your living room (or have someone else clean it for you), why not your car? Remember how wonderful it feels to get inside a nicely cleaned and vacuumed automobile where this segment of your life can be in control again.

Cleaning with intention

One simple way to transform your space and to bring it and you back to sacredness is to clean with intention. Cleaning is often relegated to the realm of drudgery, but cleaning with the intention of infusing sacredness into your surroundings brings a consciousness of purity, orderliness and renewal. If you think back to how good you feel when your house is sparkling clean and when everything is in place, you can begin to see how important it is to keep up with a cleaning routine.

Even if you don't do the cleaning yourself, a clean space can still elicit a sense of control and feelings of empowerment. This is not about making busywork in your life but it's about taking care of what you own. It's about honoring the things that are important to you. Please remember if it's not worth it to you to clean or take care of something, it's not worth keeping it in your life. If you can't bother with the simplest maintenance activities, you need to ask yourself if you really want this object. If you treasure something, you take care of it.

The very act of cleaning is a metaphor of getting the old out of your life—old negative feelings, old feelings of helplessness and vulnerability, and feelings of being out of control. Your house, of all places, needs to be the one area of your life where you have control. Try dusting just the horizontal surfaces in your space—table-tops, tops of dressers, shelves, fireplace mantels—to see what a difference it can make. Or try washing a window or two to see how clearly your vision becomes around some issue. If you take care of your space, it will take care of you.

Creating sanctuary as you travel

Traveling can provide challenges that leave you exhausted, exasperated, and less than enthusiastic to embark on another adventure. Whether business travel or even vacation travel, there are times when it's all very torturous. You are anxious to get back home into your own bed and your own familiar surroundings. Nevertheless there are times when traveling is a necessity.

For these situations, there are some simple steps you can take to ease the tension when leaving your sacred home. You take a part of it with you! You have a special bag or a little box that holds the personal things you want to take with you which you can slip into your suitcase or a carry-on bag. If you travel a lot this small bag or box may be something you have permanently assembled so it's always ready to go when you are.

In this bag can be a picture or two of your family, your pet, your house, whatever speaks to you of "home." It doesn't have to be framed. The picture or pictures can be wrapped in a silk scarf or some beautiful fabric that you use as a cloth on which to set the remembrances of home. You might have a crystal or a shell or some special token that speaks to you that you want to bring along. You also may include some incense to cleanse the room you're going to be sleeping in. A small candle will also cleanse a room if you don't want to take the chance of offending someone's allergies with incense.

When you arrive in the hotel room, spread the fabric out on top of a dresser or table and arrange the pictures, crystal, candle, etc. on the fabric You are creating a mini-sanctuary from which you draw strength and get centered. As you look at your loved ones each morning or at the end of a long business day, you remember not only why you're doing this, but also that there are those who support you and love you. Any of the items you bring should be tokens of strength and blessings for you.

Aromas enhance your intention

Realtors are giving good Feng Shui advice when they suggest that someone bake bread right before opening their home up to prospective buyers. The sense of smell can greatly enhance or deplete a space. If the aroma is pleasant, it softens up the people entering making them more receptive to what they see. But if the aroma is displeasing, people shut down and so does their perspective. Entering a home that smells of freshly baked bread is a totally different experience than entering one that smells of cat urine.

You can enhance your space with aromas in many simple ways to create a change in your life. The use of incense can bring about a change, as well as many candles that have some oils mixed right in them. When you use incense or a candle that has a pleasant smell to you, you effectively shift energy around an intention of yours. Burning a candle that emits a hint of vanilla in the Creativity area of your space reminds you of an intention that you have around opening up your creative talents and getting them moving.

Using oils in a diffuser or directly on your body can shift the tone of a space as well. If you've intentionally diffused a specific oil to assist with a difficult meeting you're facing so that you maintain clarity and self-assurance, you can also wear that same oil as a reminder of your intention. If your favorite scent is orange or lavender, you can not only incorporate it into your home but also use it directly on your body to reinforce and to remind you of your intention.

A sense of touch

One suggestion for making adjustments is to change the sense of touch in your space. Adding tactile materials, you can create a whole new feeling— velvet pillows, satin sheets, corduroy slip-covers, silk draperies, tapestries. Anything that makes you want to touch it or feel it is an appropriate way to engage this kind of adjustment. Putting suede throw pillows on an old sofa can bring about a new experience with it. Satin sheets conjure up some new images. Creamy, silk curtains can be a delicious experience. If everything has a matte finish in a room in which you want to make changes, add something glossy.

The element of touch can also be one of surprise—using some kind of material in a place where you wouldn't expect it can shift your energy very quickly. Covering doorknobs with fake fur may cause someone to be jolted into the present moment. Putting a skin-like fabric on a hand-rail when someone is expecting the usual brass or wood feel can likewise cause someone to take notice.

Another way to adjust for touch in a space is to rearrange the furniture. You can no longer "feel" your way around in the dark, but instead have to allow for a new path. Moving your furniture around is a clear statement about inviting in change. A new furniture set-up is a metaphor about taking a new path, having a new perspective, taking a new approach to something familiar. Old furniture can seem to improve with a new arrangement.

Honoring Yourself

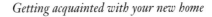

Getting acquainted with your new home

Moving into a new house is a lot like making a new friend—there's an initial time of awkwardness and uncertainty. There are certain things about the new place that are different from the old—there are different noises, different views to the outside world. Some of your things will fit beautifully and some won't. There are times when you'll be delighted that you moved and times when you figured you made a big mistake. This is all part of "getting acquainted." It becomes more dramatic if the previous owners had lived in the house for many, many years spanning all kinds of life changes—having babies, raising kids, running a business, weddings, an empty nest, deaths and finally retiring. The house may not be delighted in your invasion either, particularly if the previous owners did not adequately bring closure to their time in that space.

An effective "getting acquainted" ritual for the first few weeks you inhabit a new place is to ring the doorbell whenever you enter. This establishes your presence, states your ownership, and lets your voice be heard. If you don't like the sound of the doorbell, change it to one you love to hear. In the meantime, use a bell or a chime to announce your arrival. This Feng Shui activity can be used anytime you feel that your voice is not being heard. It will assure your authority not only to others but to yourself as well.

Bring romance into your life

A bedroom must speak to romance whether you're romancing another person or yourself. "Romance" means different things to different people. To some people romance means flowers. To others romance conjures up the image of candles—some people think of rocking chairs—for others it's a bunch of pillows, a soft blanket, a pastel color, or lace. Whatever it means to you, you need to have some element of it in your bedroom. And if you're living with a partner who will also be sleeping in that room it needs to be compatible with his/her style. If you bring in flowers because it's your favorite thing and makes you feel like the lavish, romantic and special person you are, but your partner has allergies to flowers, then another avenue needs to be explored. Both partners want to experience a feeling of romance. Using silk flowers is an option.

Many bedrooms function with a bed, a couple of dressers, and maybe a chair. It's not enough to remove anything that doesn't belong in the bedroom. You also want to bring in the "romance." Whether you enter your bedroom with a partner or by yourself, you want to be "romanced." A coat of paint in your favorite color can work wonders. In Feng Shui the color for partnerships is pink. Painting your bedroom a shade of pink or coral even if it's not in the Partnership area of your house will still change the energy. A softness can be accomplished by simply softening the color of the walls.

Maybe "romancing yourself" brings to mind a little sunny corner with a rocking chair, an afghan, and some lace curtains. Whatever it means to you, try to create it in your bedroom. This is personal space—no one else comes into your bedroom except by your invitation. So put there what you need to call in the passion you want in your life.

Enhancing an existing relationship or bringing in a new one

A relationship issue can be dramatically affected by accessing the source of this energy on the top of your desk. The Partnership area on the desk is in the back right corner from where you sit. If you want to elicit some changes in your relationship status (change one, leave one, have one), be very careful and mindful of what you place on your desk in this area.

In this back right corner, you can place a picture of you and your partner in a particularly special moment in your lives. You can have a picture of your partner alone. A separate picture of you and a separate picture of your partner speaks to division, so, unless that's your goal, it is not advisable. Anything that reminds you of growth and vitality works as a partnership adjustment. This might be a green plant or flowers. In either case, if caring for live flowers becomes inconvenient or a time problem, use silk flowers or plants. The secret is that they look alive and vital. Dried flowers are, quite bluntly, dead, and are definitely not recommended for something where you want blossoming and growth.

Lighting a candle each day in honor of your partner is thoughtful and reminds you of the "spark" between you, or rekindles that flame. Placing something in the Partnership area that your partner gave you and that you really appreciate is very auspicious—a stone, a crystal, a paperweight, a special mug. You can ask your partner to buy you a gift for this very purpose. If your partner likes to sail, a small sailboat can be a warm reminder. If your partner loves cats, a small figurine of a cat can be reminiscent of their energy.

If you want to call in a partner, a small bell might "ring" them in. Anything that portrays the sound element can be used—an angel with a horn, a pair of Chinese harmony balls, a toy instrument (perhaps an instrument the potential partner plays), or anything else your imagination creates.

Use the dining room table

The dining room table that is never used for eating except when company comes short-changes you with regard to money. If you eat and nourish your body with good food it's a metaphor for nourishing your financial life. If you never eat there, there's some money aspects that aren't happening for you. The dining room table is often abandoned to a room that now-and-again gets used—usually during the holidays or at some special family event. Otherwise the area is seldom accessed. Things are piled on the table where they'll surely be safe since no one goes in there anyway.

The dining room table is a place to eat. Using it as something else is at cross purposes to its original intention. If you hardly use the table, start using it once in a while. Imagine the feeling of fixing a special dinner for your family to eat at the dining room table as though everyone was "company." The meal becomes an event—something special has happened in your life.

You can think of your dining room table as analogous to an altar. An altar is kept clean, clear of mail and newspapers, and is treated with great reverence. You wouldn't think of spreading out a work project on an object as sacred as an altar. Your dining room table needs to assume as much importance. When it's left abandoned in a room collecting dust, money is likewise abandoning you.

Besides using it occasionally to get the money moving, activating a room that doesn't get used much is simply good luck. You want to use all parts of your house on a regular basis to keep life flowing in a smooth fashion. When stagnation occurs, things stop. Having little or no activity around the dining room table will stagnate the flow of energy we call money.

Music enhances your intentions

Musical sounds are energy and so are your thoughts. By intentionally combining the two you can create and enhance most situations. Playing music on the radio or stereo can shift energy as a Feng Shui alignment. If you're feeling like you're in a rut or can't seem to get things moving, try listening to a few marches. If you're clearing the electricity out of the air after an argument, try putting on some Debussy. By playing romantic love songs in the bedroom before a special evening, you can intentionally fill the space to reflect love and romance. If you want your teenager to do well on a test, play some Bach music in the room before studying to help with clarity.

Likewise, play some chants in your meditation room before you meditate with the intention of setting the stage for a productive experience. If you want a meeting or discussion to go well, walk around the room with a small bell holding your intention as you go. Ring it in each corner, in the center of the room, and by any furniture you may want to include. When the meeting is over you may want to do it again to clear the room. If ringing a bell may raise a few eyebrows, hum or whistle as you walk the periphery of the space. Never underestimate the power of your own voice to elicit some changes.

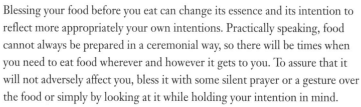

Blessing your food

Blessing your food before you eat can change its essence and its intention to reflect more appropriately your own intentions. Practically speaking, food cannot always be prepared in a ceremonial way, so there will be times when you need to eat food wherever and however it gets to you. To assure that it will not adversely affect you, bless it with some silent prayer or a gesture over the food or simply by looking at it while holding your intention in mind.

Doing a blessing before eating is a ritual many families practice anyway, often adding the element of gratitude. Any simple act that shifts the inherent energy of the food to a level of balance and harmony as well as nourishment can make significant differences in how you digest and use the food in your body. Blessing food or water for a sick person before giving it to them can ease their anxiety and help them rest better. Putting good intentions in any medication or herbs for yourself or anyone else before ingesting them will increase their effectiveness. And don't forget to bless the food you give your special pet to assure health and well-being.

Beautify the way you come in

When you come into your home through an entrance other than your front door, there are important considerations as to what you first see. Coming into a side entrance or door that enters off the garage, you usually encounter: 1) the laundry room, 2) a bathroom, 3) the kitchen, and 4) all of the above. None of these rooms provide you with the welcome you deserve. Both the laundry room and the kitchen are reminders of work to be done. The kitchen and the bathroom set the stage for health issues—digestive problems, eating disorders, weight problems. And both the laundry room and the bathroom have drains to cause your energy to be drained away when you first arrive home.

Changing the entry point is not practical nor is always trying to enter through your front door. If you enter into a back mudroom, it should be attractive and welcoming. Just because it's called a mud room doesn't means there has to be any. Don't hesitate to hang your favorite print or poster in this entrance or to paint it fun, uplifting colors. It's a crucial part of your house since the majority of time it acts as your introduction into your living space. Keep doors to bathrooms, laundry room, mechanical room, etc. closed so that you do not have to see their continual messages.

In some homes you walk *through* the laundry room, not by it. The laundry room is, in essence, the entrance you see each time you come home. It welcomes you into your space. In this case you'll have to be ever mindful to keep it picked up. Make sure you have plenty of storage space for soap, cleaners, etc. so you don't have to be looking at boxes and containers of things strewn all over. Paint it your favorite color or hang your favorite picture. When it's left unfinished or in total disarray you are not presenting a very positive message to yourself about your life or family harmony.

Honoring your car

Just like your house, your automobile will take care of you if you take care of it. Making your car as enjoyable as possible is what this is all about. When spending any amount of time in a space, the goal of Feng Shui is to make that space inviting. Keeping it clean and picked up is one simple thing to do. Automobile diffusers can be hung from the rear view mirror that emit a pleasant aroma of your choosing. Always make sure you have your favorite tapes or compact discs readily available for your use. Listening to music you love will ease the stress of driving.

Since red is such a powerful color in the Chinese tradition, tie a red ribbon on the rear view mirror or on the steering wheel for safety. Or hang a red tassel to do the same thing. Hanging any special item where you'll see it upon getting into the car can be effective as long as it doesn't obstruct your vision.

Even if you don't use your car often, seeing it as an extension of your living space emphasizes the importance of maintaining and caring for it. When buying or leasing a new or different car, take the time to cleanse it and claim it just as you would a new home. Use incense or a candle to waft through the car, both front and back seats, trunk, and around the outside. Your intention would be not only to cleanse the energy from whoever owned it before or whoever was instrumental in assembling it, but also for your safety and those who may travel with you. Or, use a small bell to do this cleansing instead, ringing it on the inside and outside of the car. Then hang the bell from the rear view mirror. Any time another cleansing seems in order, you'll have your bell handy, ready to make your automobile a supportive and safe environment.

Taking inventory

Because a closet can impact you in such a subliminal way, you can't take too many measures to assure that it works on your behalf. When dealing with a problematic closet, it's not too drastic to take everything out, mop the floor, clean or paint the walls, make sure the light bulb works, etc., etc. Once the closet is empty and ready for use, take a serious inventory of what you're storing in this closet.

Taking inventory can be painful, even wrenching, but in the end you'll experience an uplifting sense of accomplishment. Whenever you go in the closet, you'll be thrilled and proud of a job well done. Just walking by it will give you a confirmation of your self-worth. Keeping the closet in order will always be a process, but it will be easier with some semblance of order.

Since everything is energy and since everything you own has energy, you need to know what you own. Having things in your space that are of no use to you or that hold some unfortunate memories do not feed your spirit or enhance your life. In fact, they drain you of your own productivity and creativity. As boxes are filled with items, you need to have a list attached to the box or to write on the box what's inside. If there's a blank box sitting on a shelf, it will require you to constantly open it to remember what's inside. After a while that becomes very aggravating. Make an investment in what you own by knowing where it is.

Inner Wisdom

Balance in your inner life

A simplistic reduction of the principle behind Feng Shui is that when your outer space takes on a harmonious, balanced appearance, your life will begin to reflect these features. But just as it's advisable to take inventory of what you own and what you need to get rid of, it is also appropriate to take stock of what you're harboring inside, what you need to get rid of internally, and what you need to enhance.

If you think of your inner world as you would your outer, begin to apply many of the same principles of Feng Shui as in your home or office space. Compartmentalizing your life into segments—work, family, recreation—is appropriate just as your house has a room for eating, a room for sleeping, a den, a garage. To pull all these diversities together, think about a common theme that weaves them into a multi-faceted whole. In a house, you often run the same color carpet throughout. Even though the rooms hold different activities, you feel as though you can float from one to the other without a jolt in decor theme and color. The house feels like a whole.

If enthusiasm were your "carpet" that ran throughout your life, you would probably begin to see areas that need more work than other areas. Perhaps you're wildly enthusiastic about your career—you love it's challenges, what it offers you, how it stretches you. But your enthusiasm for your family life is humdrum at best. The question to ask yourself is: What can I do to bring this same amount of enthusiasm into other aspects of my life? What would it take to be as enthusiastic and excited about my family as I am about my job? Your situation may be the reverse of this, but nevertheless asking these questions in whatever framework they apply to you may bring up unpleasant issues you'll need to address. Looking at the lack of flow in your life is absolutely essential for harmonizing your inner life.

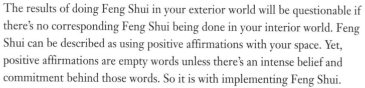

Matching inner desire and outer changes

The results of doing Feng Shui in your exterior world will be questionable if there's no corresponding Feng Shui being done in your interior world. Feng Shui can be described as using positive affirmations with your space. Yet, positive affirmations are empty words unless there's an intense belief and commitment behind those words. So it is with implementing Feng Shui.

If you're trying to make changes in the Wealth area of your house to bring in a bigger resource of cash, but all the while hold the belief that you don't deserve more money or that you already have enough, all the Feng Shui in the world won't cause that to change. Likewise, if you intentionally do some Feng Shui to ease a difficult marriage, but upon deeper examination you have to admit you don't want the marriage to work at all, the Feng Shui adjustment probably won't have much effect to bring about a happy resolution between the two of you.

What you do on the outside in your space must match what you want on the inside. Asking for the new position in your company when secretly you don't really want to do all the travel that will be asked of you as a result of this job can bring about mixed outcomes. Chances are you'll get what you asked for—the job—and then have to deal with the travel commitments which you have no interest in. Being clear and focused about what you want is critical. If you don't know what you want, then you can make use of Feng Shui to help you get clarity around an issue. It is imperative that your inner desires match the outer changes that are being made as Feng Shui adjustments.

Your heart is your inner doorway

In Feng Shui, whether inner or outer, there's an entry point which allows opportunities into your life, and projects an impression of who you are in the world. In outer Feng Shui, this entry point is your front door. In inner Feng Shui you're looking at your heart as the front door. As with your real front door, you can ask yourself many of the same questions about your heart as you'd ask about your front door, using a metaphorical meaning to interpret them.

How easy is it to get in? Does it open wide without things hidden behind it? Does it squeak and complain when being opened? Does the "handle" work? Can people easily find it or is it a hidden entry? Do you use it a lot? Do you access your space through another entrance? Do people like coming to visit? Or perhaps is your "door" hanging open all the time with no sense of boundaries or protection, susceptible to whatever walks by?

When your heart is locked tight (and no key), there's a good chance you're missing some opportunities and events. If your heart is not open or only open a little bit, what does get in is filtered by a sense of deprivation. People on the outside see this theme and react accordingly, usually not bothering to stop. In order for good luck and good fortune to get into your life, you need to open your home's front door and your heart "door."

If your heart is constricted or too vulnerable it can eventually attack your system. These "attacks" can be gentle reminders or massive blows for you to take notice and establish a better balance and flow in your life. On the other hand, when your heart is wide open, there's a need to be discerning as to what comes along.

Opening up to changes

When working on Feng Shui adjustments, it is very appropriate to clear out a space or remove some things in a specific area in which you're trying to elicit some changes. Not every corner or every table-top or every wall has to have something in it or on it. These "openings" are rest places. They allow the eye to rest and to integrate what it has already seen. Integration space is just as important as whatever else is placed in the room. Like your personal life, it's not good to be busy all the time or to have to be concentrating every minute. You need to rest; so does your space.

There's a balance between too much going on and too little. You recognize when you're too busy and trying to juggle too much in your schedule. You also recognize when you feel stagnant and when things don't seem to be moving in a fulfilling way for you. Your space also needs this balance. Identifying a cluttered, overpacked space is pretty easy. There's an overwhelming feeling when walking into the room or house. There may be a lot of furniture, a lot of plants, a lot of artwork, or all of these elements. Knick-knacks, mementos, photos can all clutter up a space. On the other side, if a space has very little in it, you can begin to feel as though you don't actually belong there. There's no personal identification and there's always the sense that your time there is temporary.

Just as you can identify the need to spend an evening at home alone with a good book, so too can your space require some restful spots. Just as you know when you need to interact with other people and do something social, your space also needs some sense of identity. When the flow and the balance are in harmony in your life and in your space, you have created good Feng Shui both inside and out.

Simplify your life

Having less simplifies your life. This is true for activities as well as for belongings. Yet it seems the busier you are, the more possessions you own. Some of these possessions were acquired in an attempt to make your life simpler—microwave, breadmaker, computer, a third car. And, while there are times when these possessions may have assisted in simplifying some activities, they often help to create more busywork in another area. Without fail you have to give more thought to using them, keeping them, maintaining them, paying for them.

It is understandable that since there's such a challenge to quiet down the inner turmoil, there will be a corresponding struggle to quiet down the outer world. When a person discovers the powerful value of getting empty on the inside, their outside world usually follows. In Feng Shui, you can begin this peaceful transition to reflect to you on a daily basis the serenity you're trying to get from within. Calming your space will help you calm your life.

Living the process

Doing Feng Shui is most effective combined with *being* Feng Shui. Although we are usually keyed into doing as much as we can for as long as we can, an important ingredient is letting the adjustments integrate and incorporate themselves into your life. Feng Shui is not about quantitative accomplishments, but about quality. If you do not take time to rest, the adjustments become too scattered. Without a pause between activities, your intention becomes diminished. Rushing from one thing to the next does not enable you to live your life with dignity.

Feng Shui, like real life, needs to be done in stages. Perhaps, after serious reflection and clarity of intent, you decide that a new partner will be welcome and appropriate. Hang a chime to reflect that intention in your Partnership area. Integrate what that chime may bring your way before you begin any other Feng Shui adjustments. Doing more does not mean getting more or getting something better. If after some time has passed, you feel you want to add to this adjustment by attaching a crystal to the chime or bringing in a plant, do it then. Doing too much too soon is counterproductive.

Feng Shui exemplifies the ebb and flow of life. Just as you go to bed when you're tired, you are active when you're rested. Thus, when you go through the activity of doing a Feng Shui adjustment, whatever it may be, there needs to be a time of "rest" or integration to allow the energy from this adjustment to begin its process. How quickly this cycle of integration moves through your life is personal. You may do one adjustment in one area of your life and your space and not feel you're ready to do another in a different area for a week or two. Others may need only a day or so to pass before they feel it's time. Whatever your process of doing Feng Shui, it's the right one. Pay attention to how you feel and make sure you're "resting."

Clean out your rooms and your problems

When a room isn't being used, it's considered bad luck in Feng Shui. Or if it's being used as a "junk room," there's a lack of flow happening in some area—something is "junked up." Likewise, from an inner sense, if there's some part of your life that's not being used, you can feel incomplete, empty or overwhelmed with a feeling of dissatisfaction (as in "Is this all there is?"). Something is not being used as it should. If your inner Feng Shui is not flowing into all areas, it's also considered bad luck.

If you were originally provided with a creative "room" that included music or art for instance, but you're no longer pursuing either of these interests, this is an area that still requires some attention from you. If your creativity is "junked up" it will affect your creative endeavors in any other areas in which you may want to use it. Of course, it doesn't make logical sense that by dusting off the guitar and playing again, you may resolve a dilemma at work. Yet this is no different than hanging a crystal in a closet to enhance your money. Everything is energy with inner and outer Feng Shui. Once your creativity is flowing, the creative muses go to work on any issues that need to be resolved.

If your Partnership "room" is being crowded out and "junked up" with anger, resentments and revenge, your partnerships will in all likelihood be filtered through these feelings. In fact, there will probably be no room for a partnership at all. Your inner Feng Shui requires that you clean out these problems and look at the issues, in order to make room for someone else.

Quick Action

Fountains add flow

Fountains are an effective Feng Shui tool because they add the elements of water, movement and sound to an environment. If there are plants growing in the fountain, that is an added feature representing life. Fountains are being used more and more in residential settings as well as corporate offices. They are no longer the large exterior systems, spewing water five feet into the air. Fountains are now available in small sizes to accommodate a table or a desk without all the consideration they used to require. Today you can buy one, put water in it, and plug it in.

All of the elements of the fountain can enhance and change life issues you want shifted. By bringing the element of water into your space you are representing the flow of money and prosperity in your life. Of course, you must keep the water clean and at an adequate level. The element of motion or the movement of the water represents for you some part of your life that perhaps isn't flowing very well. Those feelings of being stuck can be relieved with an intention in a fountain. Of course, the element of sound can bring about a peaceful recollection of some moments spent by a waterfall or a brook, listening to the relaxing sound of the water. A fountain holding your intention can manifest a lot of shifts and can get a lot of things moving in a particular area.

Selling your house

When you're going to put your house on the market there is a Feng Shui activity which can assist in the selling process. In the Helpful People area of your home, hang a chime or a crystal to beckon in both a helpful realtor who will sell your house and the prospective buyers who will bring their money to you in exchange for your house. A chime can be hung near the front door with this intention if it's in the Helpful People section. Otherwise a chime could be hung anywhere in that area. A crystal can be hung in a window in the Helpful People area with the intention of calling in the appropriate people you need to help you.

If this area is in the garage, which, if it's attached, may be the case, you can still do something to assist the sale. Once again a chime could be hung in the garage. It does not have to ring to be effective—it is your intention that "chimes" out to the universe. The color for the Helpful People area is gray. You could put something of this color in the garage to represent your intention—a gray stone, a ribbon, a gray envelope containing a piece of paper with the word "Sold" on it, a picture of your new house, or anything else that speaks to you of selling your house.

Making changes with your bed

Like the desk, your bed can be used to bring about changes that you want in life. These adjustments are placed under the bed or between the mattress and the box springs. For instance, if you want to make some changes in the Partnership area of your life, place something in the upper right hand corner as you stand at the foot of the bed. This is probably where one of the pillows is located if it's a double bed. A small stone or crystal, a love letter, or a pink ribbon can be placed under the mattress. Barring that, some thing can be placed on the floor under the bed in that area.

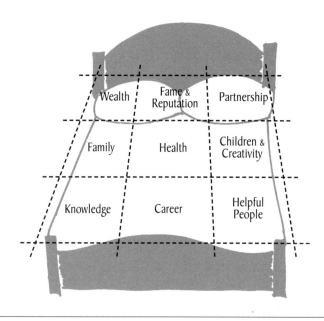

If you wanted to increase your wealth, do some corresponding adjustment in the upper left corner either under the mattress, under the bed or even under the pillow. A red envelope with a crisp new bill in it is an appropriate adjustment for money. This envelope is tucked between the mattress and the box spring with the intention of bringing in more money. A purple amethyst may also be used, or a lavender or purple ribbon, a Chinese coin—anything that says "wealth" to you.

Any career adjustments are at the foot of the bed in the middle section. In Feng Shui the color that represents this area is black. A black ribbon tied around a new bill in the denomination of your choice can represent an increase in salary. Your business card can represent your promotion within your company. Any of these items can be placed under the bed or between the mattress and box spring.

Seeing the bed as a focal point and using it to bring about some changes in your life emphasizes its importance both energetically and physically.

Flowers bring changes

Using flowers for a Feng Shui adjustment is an intense and focussed way to bring about imminent and critical change. Flowers bring beauty and life to a space but always with the understanding that they are dying. Therefore there is usually a sense of urgency around your issue when using flowers. Flowers begin to "die" as soon as they are picked so by the time they get into your space, their dying process is advanced. It is up to you not to let them wilt off their stems if you've "intentionalized" them with a desired outcome.

The Feng Shui theory with flowers is that they be used for only three days for your specific intent then replaced with fresh flowers. Repeat this cycle until you've replaced them a total of nine times. This particular adjustment requires a very strong and pointed attention on your intention which is why it is so effective for an impending change. If someone in your family suddenly becomes quite ill, bring flowers into the center of the house (where health is located) and replace them every third day nine times in a row. This elicits a considerable effort on your part. When a job offer is on the line, place flowers in the Career area to energize the issue beyond simply placing a vase with silk flowers in it.

The flowers that have been replaced can be moved to other parts of the house but not "re-intentionalized" around some other matter. They are simply moved and enjoyed for their beauty until removed permanently.

Flowers force you to stay with an issue by requiring you to deal with their status on a regular basis. Each time you shop for flowers, replace old ones, and put in new ones, you bring your attention back to the matter at hand. Unlike other adjustments which, once they're in place, you only need to clean or water once in a while, flowers due to their fragility demand we recognize them, take care of them, and take care ourselves.

Pets add life

When your life feels stagnant or "in a rut," a pet can add the spark you're looking for. Anyone who has had the experience of owning a pet knows the "life" an animal can bring to a space. Animals are, by nature, from the fire element in the Chinese Five Element system. Naturally they bring a spark to wherever they live and with whom they live. A dog or a cat obviously can add some fire to your life. Even a pet that doesn't seem to take up much space or require an inordinant amount of your attention can affect your outlook—a bowl of goldfish, gerbils in a cage, a parakeet.

Whether you want to add some zip to one element of your life or to your whole life, a pet can assist in this process. Placing a birdcage with two small birds in the Relationship area of your home can enliven your marriage or significant partnership—the two birds representing a couple. A hamster placed in the Career area of your bedroom or of your office may begin to put your career on a fast-track. An aquarium filled with beautiful fish can help to attract money into your life. In Feng Shui, money and water are always connected. Likewise an energetic new puppy or a mischievous little kitten can undoubtedly enliven not just one area of your life but every aspect as it runs through your house.

Sometimes you don't even know the "life" a pet has provided until it's gone. A beloved animal can help to keep you focused when you're feeling particularly scattered, or they can bring a sense of calmness when you're agitated. They can get you moving at a certain time in your day or at a certain place in your life when you would otherwise fall into your usual predictable routine.

Pets can help

An uncaged pet who is left to run free throughout your space will affect all aspects of your life. A rambunctious, playful dog who runs all over your house will inevitably bring about changes in your life. A mischievous kitten leaves no part of your life/space untouched. If you want some monumental things to shift for you, get a pet if you don't already have one. If you don't want your pet to be in certain areas of your house or in certain rooms, look to see what areas you're "defending." It isn't necessary that your pet have full range to do whatever they want wherever they want. But notice which rooms you are declaring off-limits to their "fire" and their inevitable upheaval.

Even though a pet may spread its energy all over your space, you can still specify some changes in just certain areas of your life. You can "nest" or "headquarter" a pet in a particularly relevant spot to symbolize some changes you want to manifest. For instance, you can make up your dog's bed or kennel in the Children and Creativity area to lift stagnation around some creative endeavor in which you're involved. You might try making up an irresistible hide-away in which the cat can nap in the Helpful People area of your bedroom if you're trying to sell your house or plan a trip. Resting or asleep, your pet can bring some shift in energy to an area. A slow-moving pet iguana or a very wise old cat who sleeps most of the day can add a significant vibration of fire and movement to your life.

A pet can assist you in many transitions throughout your life. Incorporating them in your intentions will not only increase the magnitude of your intention but will provide you with a loving protector as well.

Working with outside animals

Sometimes we need to bring in the animal nature in ways other than a pet. Allergies, living restrictions, or time restrictions, indicate that a pet may not fit into your lifestyle. Animals can still be part of your life if you attract them outside. A birdfeeder outside the Children and Creativity area of your home will bring you plenty of birds and plenty of activity and good fortune with creative endeavors. A birdfeeder outside a Wealth area can bring blessings in that aspect. A birdbath in the Partnership area of your garden can enhance a relationship, particularly if you're looking to bring someone into your life. Birds of any kind are very fortuitous. Attracting them to your garden or yard are beneficial.

Just like a puppy inside your space, you can work with the animal kingdom in your yard to bring about changes you want. Squirrels, chipmunks, rabbits, frogs, butterflies all bring good luck. Animals come to a place that holds good energy and reinforce it. Strategically placing birdbaths, feeders, fountains, ponds, or special flowers, you can bring activity to an area that needs new life. If you're ever blessed to have deer walk upon your land, you can experience their special qualities of strength, gentleness, and beauty. Watch where they walk—usually they follow some strong energy fields coming up from the ground. See if there's any relevance to some aspects in your life. Perhaps you could attract them to linger in the Career area of your yard by putting food out for them in that spot. Add to the food your intention of tapping into their intelligence around any career issues.

Planting special flowers that attract butterflies with the intention of getting your name out into the community can bring expansive results. A birdhouse in the Children and Creativity area may help to nurture your inner child at its bleakest, coldest moments. Having a heated birdbath during the winter months in the Health area can help to assure your well being.

Mistletoe can be surprising

Mistletoe used during the holidays can be an effective Feng Shui adjustment for some problematic features. Hung from the ceiling in a little cluster, its traditional intention is to elicit a kiss for anyone who stands under it. If positioned with some intention behind it, it can be functional and fun.

When hung somewhere between a front door that is directly aligned to the back door, it can act as a barrier between the two so that the ch'i or energy doesn't come in and go out too quickly. Hang it from the ceiling halfway between the two doors to slow the energy down. If the kitchen is the first thing you see upon entering your home, hang some mistletoe in the archway leading into the kitchen. It will draw your attention away from the tendency to want to snack as soon as you get home. Instead, you will look for nurturance in the form of a kiss.

Because mistletoe is one of those items that causes a reaction, it can be effective to raise the energy in the Partnership area of your home. If hung with intention it can represent to you the excitement of a new relationship or the renewal of an existing one. Mistletoe hung in the center of your house can hold the intention of love for your family and for the world. No matter where you decide to put your holiday mistletoe, it's sure to hold some surprises and fun-loving good cheer.

The powerful color of red

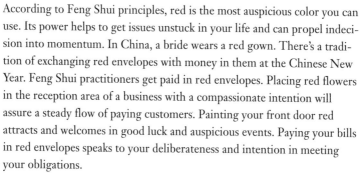

According to Feng Shui principles, red is the most auspicious color you can use. Its power helps to get issues unstuck in your life and can propel indecision into momentum. In China, a bride wears a red gown. There's a tradition of exchanging red envelopes with money in them at the Chinese New Year. Feng Shui practitioners get paid in red envelopes. Placing red flowers in the reception area of a business with a compassionate intention will assure a steady flow of paying customers. Painting your front door red attracts and welcomes in good luck and auspicious events. Paying your bills in red envelopes speaks to your deliberateness and intention in meeting your obligations.

Even wearing red can put you into a very outward flow of energy for those times when you need to take command of a situation or to feel more empowered. Wearing even the smallest amount of red lifts your energy. A small red lapel pin will remind you of your fire. The color does not even have to be seen in order for its effect to take hold. Wearing a red slip or red underwear can be even more effective because the color is closest to your skin. Any time you can incorporate or wear the color red, it assists the flow of events that might otherwise take longer to happen or that may never happen at all.

Connecting to
Your House

A letter to your house

When your living space becomes "alive" to you, you establish a connection not only to your home but also to your own life. When you truly see what a mirror your space offers you, resolving dilemmas, addressing difficult situations and lessening problems can be a real possibility through the assistance of your home. Connecting to your space is the piece that is often overlooked or discounted—maybe because there's no obvious procedure for how to make this connection. Maybe because making this connection requires a leap of faith.

Making a connection with your house doesn't require that you like the space or that it provides you with wonderful memories. Your home may not have been problem-free. Perhaps it has presented many opportunities to practice patience, endurance, and fortitude. The first connection with your space is to write it a letter. Address it in whatever way feels appropo: "Dearest House" or "To My Charming Little Apartment" or "Dear Money-Pit."

Begin by telling your space what you think of it. Your letter does not by any means have to be a litany of accolades or praises for what a good job it's been doing. If things have been lousy, say so. If it has provided you with warmth and harmony, be sure to express these sentiments with gratitude. Share your expectations with your home, what you hope to accomplish there and where you're headed in life. Express features you're planning to restore or remodel in the future. Acknowledge shortcomings on your part: "I'm sorry I didn't get the front door fixed before it blew off in the storm." "I feel badly that I didn't get around to painting the living room walls sooner now that I see how beautiful it looks." Write as though you're talking to a close friend. Who accepts your activities and habits better than your home? Keep the letter in a journal so you can add to it as you feel drawn to do so.

Drawing your house

Besides writing to your home, you can also spend a few moments and draw what your home means to you. Gather together some paper and markers of different colors. Find a place preferably within your house where you won't be disturbed for a few minutes. Sit quietly for a moment or two to get in touch with how you feel about your current home. This doesn't require artistic skill but it does require some concentration and effort. Drawing your home to some people may mean literally drawing the shape of the house, the front door, the sidewalk, any trees, etc., etc. The drawing may become more of a floor plan where you draw the different rooms, the doors, some of the furniture. "Home" may also mean your bedroom because it's the only place in which you feel "at home." Or it could mean a porch or a reading area, or the swing in the backyard or the garden.

Drawing your home could also be expressed in a more right brain fashion with color and shapes that have no realistic representation of a house, yours or anyone else's. If you feel a lot of anger and resentment as to what has happened during your time in this space, you may take a red marker and depict your anger in zig-zag strokes sweeping across the page. You may feel yellow flower-like shapes best represents the softness and love you've felt living in this home.

Doing this drawing exercise after having just written a letter to your living space is appropriate because you're already in the energy of your home. It is important that no one else see what you've drawn unless you choose to share it. Keep this drawing in your journal where you can access it from time to time. Any subsequent drawings can be added to it as time passes.

Write to the home where you grew up

You may find that connecting to your house on a regular basis can provide you with answers and guidance for issues not only dealing with the house itself (Should we add on a porch? Would it be okay to remodel the back bedroom?) but also with other issues in your life (Is this a good time to nurture a new relationship? Where is my money going?). Writing to your house is like finding a new friend who knows you intimately and who has your best interests at heart. The mistake is when you believe the house has a vendetta against you. When it seems that everything has needed repair, appliances have failed, roofs have leaked and doors have stuck, it doesn't usually mean that your home is mad at you. It only reflects what's going on in your own life—getting mad at your house is a diversion from having to look at what's making you angry about your own issues. Don't blame your house for bad luck!

Besides writing to your home regularly, an exercise that can provide valuable insight into your current situation is to write to the home in which you lived as a child. The home you remember having grown up in often holds a similar pattern to where you're currently living. Tell that home what you liked best about it and what was most challenging about living there. This doesn't necessarily mean what structural features you liked or didn't like, but it does mean what about your life you liked or didn't like while you were living there.

If you moved a lot as a child and don't have one particular house you could call "home," then use a past space you've lived in as an adult. Making a comparison between where you are now and where you were earlier in your life gives you a baseline. You can see if the same issues you were experiencing as a young adult or as a child are still in your life. The information you get from this comparison are critical for any changes you're trying to elicit in your life now.

Create the home you want in your mind

After writing to your house and drawing what your house represents to you, you may come to the realization that there's no place to go where you feel "at home." There's no room or corner or even a small hide-away like a closet that provides you the kind of privacy and safety you need. When your home doesn't seem to provide you the nurturing you need, then you'll need to create it. In order to create it in your home, you'll need to create it in your mind. This process will take some reflective time thinking about what "home" means.

Find a time in your schedule when you are assured of no interruptions. If that won't happen in your house, then go to a coffee shop or a library or book store where you can reflect and take notes if needed. Once you're settled in your quiet spot, take a few deep breaths. Let go of the day and any concerns and worries that have been plaguing you. Be assured that when you leave this spot you'll be better able to deal with what's waiting for you. This is where you need to be now.

As you begin this journey within, be aware that your goal is to find the most sacred spot for you and you alone. It may be a space you knew as a child or it may be a brand new situation that could hold some surprises for you. Leave yourself open to whatever images you get. There is no right or wrong place—it only needs to meet your criteria. Begin by finding yourself standing in front of a door or gate. You may see yourself walking up to the door/gate, noticing its color, its height, what it's made of. When you walk through that doorway you will be in your sacred spot—the place in all the world that you can be in to simply just *be*. It's a place where you can let down your shoulders, relax, breathe, and be quiet. Write down what you see and what feelings come to you.

See and feel that home in your mind

Once you get into your imagined sacred space, it is important that you not only take notice of how you feel but also how the space looks. You may want to re-create this place or some aspects of it in your own real world. Notice if you feel "nested." Can you breathe easily? Is there a sense of uneasiness or do you feel completely safe and alone? Are you charmed by this place? Write down your feelings as you go, while you create this space in your mind.

Now begin noticing the physical characteristics. Are you indoors or outside? Is your sacred space a garden? A forest? A treehouse? A room? An attic? Have you been here before? Notice the colors around you. Is there a place to sit? A chair? A sofa? A bed? Take note of the size of the room and the height of the ceilings. Are there any animals nearby? If there's anything you want to change about your space, you can do that now. You can change the color of the walls, the floor covering, the lighting as you wish. If your sacred spot is in a cave but you want running water or electricity, you can do that. This is your vision—anything is possible. Jot down the features that appeal to you as you encounter them.

Sit or be in different parts of the space to get different perspectives. Is one area more comfortable than another? If candles are your favorite form of lighting, don't worry about whether the candles will burn out or how many you'll need to get the lighting effect you want. The candles will be just the way you want them. Notice the temperature. Are there any smells you notice? Keep only those that are pleasing to you. When you think you've gotten the space just right, languish in it. Take it all in. Hold the peace and gratitude in your heart. Be prepared to bring those heart feelings back with you. Write down any other thoughts and experiences you have had while in your space.

Next, find that quiet central spot

The purpose of finding or creating a space in your imagination is that you begin to see what your heart requires to get to a quiet central spot. Your notes and memory are a reference. Gather some paper and markers to draw your space. Again this could be a literal interpretation of what you saw. If you were in a log cabin, draw the inside with the fireplace and any furniture you want to include. Or, your drawing may be a loose rendition of how you felt there. If you felt in harmony with yourself and the world, your drawing may be a series of circular shapes or softer, more flowing forms. Compare your drawing of your current house with the drawing of your sacred space.

As you become aware of this sacred place to which you can go any time you want, you may find yourself trying to "bring back" elements of this favorite little corner to incorporate into your physical reality. You may want to paint your bedroom a darker, more intense color after realizing that a cave gives you the security you're looking for. You may want to finish a long overdue landscape project when you realize that your heart longs to spend time in a garden. A fountain may find its way into your house after you heard the sound of water flowing in your sacred space.

Being mindful of what your innermost soul needs is how you create sacred space. This space may never become a reality. You can still "visit" there whenever you want and you can stay as long as you need to. The benefit to this kind of an inner sacred place is that it is very easy to rearrange things and to change its look—affordable, too! The more you go there, the more clarity you will have around what works and what doesn't work for you in your own home. If a room, an object or a lifestyle doesn't support those innermost feelings, you change it or get rid of it. Once you identify what your innermost soul needs, nothing else will suffice.

Listen to your space

When you listen to your space, you can connect to its music. A house holds all kinds of instruments that provide you with resonances that become familiar and almost unheard: the refrigerator, the furnace, a fan, the air conditioner, or a computer. These appliances will run almost like white noise—there, but not recognized. When you sit and listen in your home, you not only hear the obvious things but you also begin to hear the percussive sounds that pervade on an intermittent basis. A door that creaks, a faucet being turned on and off, a toilet being flushed, the sound of the oven. All of these add to the fullness of the house.

To spend a few minutes actively listening in the middle of your house or a room may provide you with a level of familiarity in your home that you've been missing. It's easy to know what a room looks like but to ask yourself what it sounds like brings with it a deeper intimacy. All of the sounds, whether ongoing or a now-and-then occurrence, provide an orchestral harmony that makes up your space. Everything comes in on cue, never missing a beat. Listening to the symphony brings you to a deeper understanding of your house and yourself.

When you listen to your space, you can connect to its heartbeat. The more you practice listening, the more you will pick up on the subtleties and obscure elements of your home. All of the sounds are part of what it is. None are good or bad. You wouldn't think to eliminate all B-flat notes from the symphony you're listening to because suddenly you feel they aren't as good as some of the other notes—it's part of the whole piece. Every note has a purpose. Likewise every sound has a purpose, an element of lifeforce that creates the beat in the heart and in the music.

Index

The Beginning

Just as the end is close at hand, the seeds of a new beginning start to expand. Although the pages of *Wind and Water: Your Personal Feng Shui Journey* have ended, your personal Feng Shui journey has only begun.

As you incorporate many of the suggestions throughout this book, you will become aware that your life is somehow different. You will take stock of your possessions and of how you relate to them. Your living and working space will have new importance as you look at the meaning they hold for you. Feng Shui does that.

Your journey will be personal, however, so some of the general suggestions in this book may not integrate into your space. If you have questions, comments, or require a consultation, please feel free to contact me. We can experience the journey together, creating sacred space for both of us.

Carole J. Hyder
901 W. Minnehaha Parkway
Minneapolis, MN 55419
612-823-5093
email: hyder@goldengate.net